Heads Up

Heads Up

Carol Meldrum

D&C
David and Charles

www.rucraft.co.uk

Contents

Introduction

There are plenty of hair accessories available in the stores but if you want to stand out from the crowd, why not make your own? It really couldn't be easier. The 21 projects featured in this book include all the possibilities — clips and grips, headbands and hair combs, tiebacks and garlands. The decorative elements are interchangeable giving you the chance to pick and mix, to dip in and out, and to come up with your own combinations. *Heads Up* will inspire your creativity and encourage you to find and develop your own individual style.

Making your own hair accessories is a great way to sample all sorts of crafts, from knitting and crochet, to beading and wirework, as well as simple sewing and embroidery. Working on these designs has given me a chance to revisit and re-ignite my love of all things craft and I hope the same is true for you. The range of projects has been created with both beginners and more experienced crafters in mind, so whether you are starting out on your creative journey or want to brush up on existing skills, there is something here for you.

You may have many of the materials and equipment you will need already, more than likely leftover from other creative endeavours. In fact you are positively encouraged to recycle, rework and re-use. Soon you will start to look at scraps of fabric, buttons and beads in an entirely different light. There is a real treasure trove of ideas for transforming the different elements into fabulously unique hand-crafted accessories.

Start by looking through the photo catalogue of projects at the beginning of the book, make your choice, then turn to Making the Projects for the how-to instructions for each design. Some of the projects have more than one variation, and the design inspirations provided give you even more ideas for exploring the creative possibilities. There is also a short techniques section to provide extra help.

I genuinely hope you get as much enjoyment from this book as I did putting the ideas together, and remember, handmade doesn't have to look home-made. Treat the projects as serving suggestions — add a sprinkle of imagination and a touch of inspiration to make each design your own. Have fun, experiment and enjoy the journey!

MATERIALS AND EQUIPMENT

The projects have been designed to encourage you to recycle and re-use existing materials, from fabrics to buttons. Many of the designs use basic hair accessories such as clips, grips and bands as a foundation base, so get ready to rework your discarded pieces. The tools required are basic and the chances are that you will already have most of them around the house.

EVERYDAY BASICS

If you are missing any of the basics, they can be easily purchased; aim to build up your resources as you work through the designs.

Scissors

You'll need a small sharp pair for cutting embroidery threads, a large pair of dress-making scissors for cutting fabrics, and a pair of craft scissors for cutting out templates and fine craft wire.

Cutting wire or paper will blunt scissors so never be tempted to use your dress-making scissors for these activities.

Sewing needles

Sharp or standard sewing needle These are used to sew up fabric or to attach hair combs and clips, etc., to a fabric base.
Tapestry needle This has a blunt point and a large eye and is used for sewing in ends of yarn on knitting/crochet projects.
Embroidery needle For the adding of embroidered embellishments, this type of needle has a long thin eye; the head of the needle is usually narrow and flat allowing it to move easily through the fabric.

Sewing thread

You will probably want to have a selection of colours available, and black and white threads are your essentials.

When choosing a colour to match your chosen fabric, as a rule of thumb it is best to go for a slightly darker shade; check the colour in daylight as artificial light can change the colour dramatically.

Always take a piece of the fabric you are matching when going to the store to buy thread – never rely on your memory.

Glue

Make sure the glue you use is suitable for the type of project you are making, for example if you need to attach something to a metal base, check the manufacturer's instructions to ensure that the glue is up to the job. In fact it may well be worth investing in a glue gun.

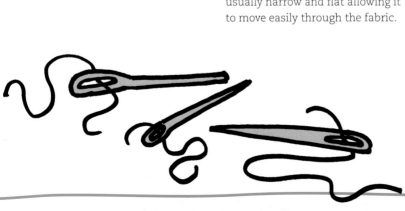

Using a glue gun

The glue comes in the form of a stick which is pushed through the heated gun when you squeeze the gun trigger. Make sure the gun is switched on for a few minutes before using to allow the glue to soften and melt, and protect your work surface with a heat-proof covering.

Other essentials

Tape measure Choose one that has both centimetres and inches on the same side.

Ruler A clear plastic ruler is ideal for marking out any shapes or lines onto your fabric.

Steam iron and ironing board You'll need these to remove creases from fabric before cutting, and for fixing folds and bonding fusible webbing/interfacing to stiffen fabrics.

Glass-headed pins Make sure the pins you use are rust-proof to avoid marking your fabric; avoid plastic or pearl-headed pins as they can melt if ironed; always use a pin with a brightly coloured head so they are easy to see.

Elastic For making your own bands for several of the projects, you will need a 9mm (³/₈in) wide general-use braided elastic, which is available in either black or white.

Notebook This ensures you keep all your design ideas in one place rather than scribbling down your creative inspirations on scraps of paper to be misplaced or lost.

If your tape measure is old and frayed, consider replacing it as it is likely to have stretched and may no longer measure accurately.

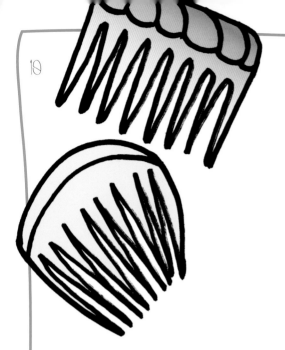

HAIR ACCESSORIES

Many of the projects in this book use basic shop-bought hair accessories as the base for the designs. These are cheap to buy and are easily purchased from accessory stores and chemists.

Hair combs

These are available in different sizes and colours: choose a clear hair comb if you want the comb to blend into the hair and a tinted one if the comb is meant to be seen as part of the design. Usually made of moulded plastic or metal, combs have a bar running along the top and teeth coming down from the bar. Most are slightly curved to allow them to sit snugly on the head.

Hair grips

Hair grips (aka kirby grips and bobby pins) are available in a variety of colours to match different hair shades. The standard length is approx. 5cm (2in)

but longer grips are available up to about 7cm (2¾in). Most grips have a slight kink or wave in them to help them to stay in place, as well as covered ends to avoid them snagging in the hair.

Hair clips

There are lots of different types of clip available but I have chosen to use just two different styles as I find these make the best bases for decorating. **Click clacks** (aka sleepies) An elongated oval shape that when closed is slightly curved to allow it to sit flat on the head. This type of clip is available in many different lengths and colours. **Sectioning clips** (aka duck-bill clips) Long and narrow, with a spring clip at one end and tapered to a blunt point at the other. They are made of metal and again are slightly curved.

Headbands

The headbands (aka Alice bands) used for the projects have all been covered with fabric as a starting base for the designs (see Techniques: Covering a Headband). Headbands are made of plastic or metal to give them slight ease and to ensure one size fits all. They are available in different widths, although the projects featured use only 5mm (¼in) and 1.5cm (⁵/₈in) widths.

The uncovered bands have small raised teeth on the underside to help grip the hair and keep the headband in place. Although the teeth are covered up when you apply the fabric, the band will still sit perfectly on the head.

Headbands designed for children will also fit an average adult head.

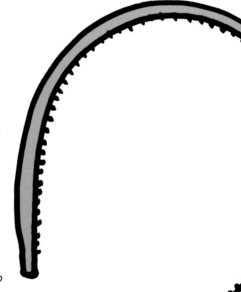

FABRIC

The word fabric is used as a generic term, covering a wide variety of textiles and cloths. Fabric is constructed from threads or yarn and can be woven, knitted/crocheted, or created by pressing fibres together. You need not be bound to the fabric choices I have made for the projects in this book, and you are encouraged to experiment.

Felt fabric

Felt fabric is available in lots of different colours and can be found in most fabric, haberdashery and craft stores. It can be bought by the metre/yard or in pre-cut rectangles.

Felt is constructed from fibres that have been pressed together so it does not fray or need hemming, making it ideal for the types of project featured in this book. As it is slightly thick it keeps its shape, making it a great base for adding embellishments and decoration to.

Patchwork cotton

Designed for making patchwork quilts, the range available, both plain or printed, make these light-weight woven fabrics ideal. Back the fabric with fusible webbing/interfacing to stiffen it and to reduce its tendency to fray, and hem the edges to prevent fraying. Patchwork cotton can be bought by the metre/yard or in fat quarters (a quarter metre/yard of fabric cut in a square rather than a narrow strip). You can also buy charm packs with 15cm (6in) squares of different fabric colours/prints selected to coordinate, making them perfect for smaller projects such as hair accessories.

Dress-making cotton

Dress-making cotton is very similar to patchwork cotton and can be found in different weights. For the finer weights it is best to back them with fusible webbing/interfacing; while heavier weights do not drape so much and therefore may not need backing, they will need to be hemmed. These fabrics are available in an endless variety of patterns and colours.

I have found that natural fibres work best or fabrics with a slight synthetic blend (polycottons).

Adding body to fabric

It may be necessary to stiffen your chosen fabric to make it easier to cut out and work with. This is achieved by backing the fabric with fusible webbing and interfacing.

Fusible webbing (aka Bondaweb) An iron-on fabric adhesive that can be purchased by roll or in handy pre-cut pieces; it is used to join fabric pieces. A hot iron is required to fuse/bond the fabrics together.

Interfacing A non-patterned fabric used to stiffen or thicken another fabric. It can be sewn or bonded together and is available in different weights depending on how stiff you require the fabric to be.

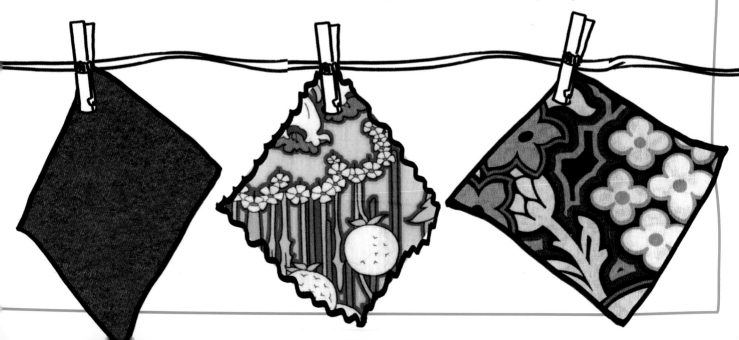

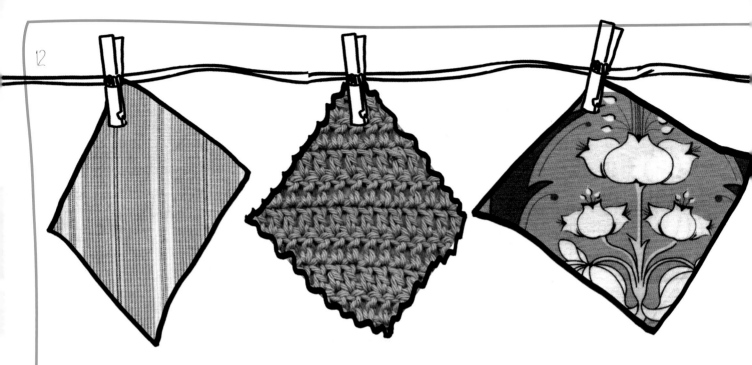

Using reclaimed fabric

Hair accessory projects are a perfect way to give old garment fabrics a new lease of life. Start by looking through your wardrobe for clothes that are past their best. Charity stores and jumble sales are also great places to rummage around to find discarded gems.

- Old faded denims are always fun to play with.
- Leather is great as it won't fray, but for thicker leather fabrics you may need to use a special leather needle if stitching is required.
- T-shirts and fine jersey weights are stretchy knitted fabrics. They will roll up and fray when you cut them so be aware of this; also check the fibre content as 100% acrylic can melt if you apply heat to it.

Why stop at fabric? Reclaim, buttons, beads, sequins, zips and trims too.

Choosing your fabric

When choosing your fabric, remember that you will only be using a very small section for most of the projects. Here are a few things to think about.

Plain/patterned fabrics

- Think about the scale of pattern and how it will work with your chosen fabric.
- A plain fabric might need some embellishment.

Knitted fabric

- You can always incorporate the fraying effect of this fabric into your design.
- Heavy-weight machine and hand-knit fabrics are generally too thick for the projects in the book.

Several of the featured projects have a knitted or crocheted base; if you are a beginner, turn to the Techniques section.

Ribbon and trims

Ribbons are used to make some of the projects and the width and type has been specified, but you can easily choose an alternative to give the projects a different look.

Double satin A versatile ribbon that is shiny and smooth on both sides.

Organdy/Organza A sheer, woven-fabric ribbon that has a luxurious look.

Tartan/Gingham Distinctive patterned woven-fabric ribbons.

Petersham/Grosgrain Thick corded woven ribbons.

Velvet Ribbon that has a thick short pile on one side.

Wired This is a light-weight ribbon that has wire hemmed into its edges so it can be bent and twisted into shape.

Lace trim A net-like ornamental trim that can be made from cotton or nylon.

If a project requires heat to be applied to the fabric, test a small section first.

EMBELLISHMENTS

All sorts of embellishment can be added to your hair accessories from buttons and beads to sequins and stitchery. Here are the items you may need to embellish the projects, depending on the designs you choose to make.

Embroidery threads

A selection of projects have been embellished using decorative embroidery stitches. There are a selection of threads available that can be used, but I have used stranded cotton (floss). This comes in skeins made up of six strands loosely wound together that can be split down to the required thickness. I have generally used two strands but you can add more if you desire a thicker appearance. Alternatively, simply separate strands from yarns that you would normally use for knitting or crochet, but never split yarn to less than two strands as a single strand will easily break with very little pulling.

For advice on working the decorative embroidery stitches see Techniques.

Buttons

I have often utilized buttons in the designs, for flower centres and as decorations in their own right. Both shop-bought and reclaimed flat-back buttons have been used, as well as woven and self-cover buttons.

Flat-back buttons

These have either two or four holes for attaching. Buttons made from natural materials, such as shell or horn,

will vary in texture and colour while moulded plastic and metal buttons will have a more uniform appearance.

When using shop-bought or reclaimed buttons hunt around for interesting ones that will enhance your project.

Shank buttons

This type of button has a loop at the back for attaching. I have used two different types:
Woven buttons A moulded plastic button specially designed with canvas-like sections for weaving yarn or thread in and out of; the idea is to fill in the sections to cover the plastic base.
Self-cover buttons These are available in metal and plastic in a range of different sizes, although for the projects included in this book the metal ones are recommended, as the shank is removed from the button back to make it flat to allow it to be glued to a flat surface.

Beads and sequins

These are a great way to add a touch of sparkle to a project. There are lots of different choices available to you and I have used the following:
Seed beads This is the generic term used for any small bead; they are usually made of glass and are available in a variety of sizes. The

most common shape is round, but they are also available in other shapes such as a droplet or cube. Seed beads are usually sold by weight.

Bugle beads These are also classed as a seed bead as they are small in size, but their shape is completely different. They are long and tubular-shaped with flat sides, and they too are available in a variety of lengths, colours and finishes.

Freshwater pearls These have a beautiful lustre, iridescence and high-quality finish. They are available in a variety of sizes, although as they are a natural product the shapes are often irregular and this adds to their beauty.

Sequins These come in a variety of shapes, sizes and finishes. Although I have used only flat sequins, you could easily choose something different such as cupped or novelty-shaped ones. As sequins are usually made of plastic, it is best to avoid applying any sort of heat to them as they may become misshapen.

Working with beads

Beads can be either stitched or wired onto hair accessories, depending on the project you choose.

- Make sure the bead hole is large enough to fit through the wire or thread being used.
- Always buy more beads than the project instructions state as you may find that some are misshapen, or get broken or lost.
- Discard beads that have sharp edges to avoid snagging the fabric or you; this can be a particular problem with bugle beads.
- When stitching on beads, use a doubled thread for extra strength. When wiring on beads, use a plated wire for the highest finish. Plated means

that the copper or nickel base has been coated to give it the look of a precious metal. If this proves too expensive, craft wires are available in lots of different colours.

- Wire size is expressed as a gauge (e.g. 24-gauge) or in millimetres (e.g. 1.2mm); note, the larger the gauge and the smaller the 'mm', the finer the wire.
- For cutting and twisting wire, round-nose pliers are best.

Craft feathers

You can find many different sorts of feathers in most good craft and haberdashery stores, although a more extensive range can be found online. Craft feathers can either be natural or dyed, and they tend to come from guinea fowl, chickens and turkeys. They can be bought in bags or, for the more fancy types, in strips or in bunches bound together.

Loose feathers can be slightly tricky to work with as the slightest draught will make them fly about, and you will need to be careful and patient. It can help if you select feathers that have a longer stem running down the centre, as this will make it easier to pin them onto the project and allow you to stitch them in place without trapping or flattening the fibres.

BUTTON COLLECTION

For a hair accessory that is as bright as a button, display your favourite fasteners on this fabulous fascinator...

... or make your very own woven buttons — plastic button bases can be decorated with yarn or embroidery thread to coordinate with just about anything.

BEADED
BEAUTY

What better way to
add a sparkle to your
day than with this
beaded hair comb?

VINTAGE FEATHERS

For style and sophistication, this 1950s-inspired fascinator can't be beaten.

OVERSIZED FLOWER

One design, two great looks! For the fabric flower, I've chosen brightly coloured bold and busy prints for the petals and embellished it with a beaded centre.

For the felt flower, I've selected hot pinks and purples with a touch of red, adding a dark feather trim and rainbow bead border to achieve that Spanish Flamenco look.

BAND OF BUTTONS

The answer to your prayers — a multi-layered flexible headband that won't slip off your head after just a few minutes!

NORTHERN PLAINS
PUBLIC LIBRARY
Ault, Colorado

FLAPPER STYLE

Inspired by the 1920s, the feather headband has been brought bang up to date and right on trend with two great designs.

TAKE A BOW

What a scoop — a simple shop-bought band is given a spectacular makeover with this tartan ribbon treatment.

TRIO OF ROSES

Stand out from the crowd with this headband decorated with simple-to-make rolled fabric roses. Be as imaginative as you like with your fabric selection.

NAUTICAL
CHIC

Keep your hair
ship-shape at all
times with these
stylish gold and
silver headbands.

GLITTERYGLAMOUR For vintage chic decorate a simple hair clip with a stunning beaded circle.

MINIATURE ROSES

The kirby grip is a basic essential whatever your hair length. Transform this simple grip into a tiny work of art with a perfectly formed miniature rose.

FLOWER
CUT OUTS

Zone in on flower
fabric prints to create
these super little
3D clips that stand
out in a crowd.

COVER UP

Covered buttons are so versatile and the customizing possibilities are almost endless. Here I have used a set of three different sizes to jazz up the simplest hair clips.

PRETTY KNITTY FLOWERS

These cute little floral hair grips are a great way to add a splash of colour to your day, and they can be crocheted or knitted (as shown overleaf) — the choice is yours.

Whether you decide on bright jewel-like tones, or a palette of mellow autumnal shades, these little crochet flowers are blooming beautiful.

PRETTY KNITTY FLOWERS

Knit yourself up a blast
of botanic to keep long
hair out of your eyes.

PAISLEY
PANACHE

This sparkly clip is quite a show piece, but it can be easily dressed up or played down to suit your own look.

RIBBON ROSE GARLAND

This beautiful garland is the best way to hippy chic for the festival season, made with ribbon roses and gold braid, you'll whip it up in a jiffy!

BEAD MOSAICS

The beaded grips opposite are simple and straightforward to make. The circular layered motif gives you a great base to work a selection of stitches and a medley of beads.

SUPERSNUGTIEBACK

Made from a knit or crochet fabric, these terrific tiebacks have a little bit of stretch to sit snugly in place without sliding off your head, as bands made of elastic so often do. Decorate as you choose — I used a few crochet flowers and felt leaves for the knitted version and a large rolled rose for the crocheted one pictured opposite.

FAB
FABRIC
TIEBACKS

The fabric tieback is a fashion necessity and I have given you two to choose from — the curvy broad band and the simple straight skinny band.

WOVEN WONDERS

These crochet headband sleeves are fantastic; simply by changing the woven insert they can look chic or street all within the blink of an eye. Be clever with your colour choice to create an accessory that will take you from day to night.

DAISY CHAIN

Recreate the daisy chains of your childhood for the perfect summer party garland. Each flower is made individually, and the daisies are then simply slotted together to make the garland.

MAKING THE PROJECTS

BUTTON COLLECTION

Hair combs make the perfect base for these fun fascinators decorated with beautiful buttons. Choose from the quick and easy bought button fascinator or the little more creative woven button fascinator.

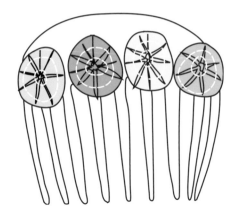

Materials

For the bought button fascinator
- Hair comb
- Buttons: three large, three small

For the woven button fascinator
- Hair comb
- Four creative buttons (see Suppliers)
- Cord elastic
- 4ply (fine-weight) yarn: small amounts in four different colours
- White embroidery thread

Making the bought button fascinator

Place a small button on top of a large button, and stitch together using a complementary thread.

Using a glue gun or super glue, add a small drop of glue to the centre of the underside of one of the button stacks. Place a small drop of glue to the top of the comb where you want to position the first button and press on the button stack; hold the two tightly together until the glue has bonded. Repeat the gluing process for the remaining buttons.

Set the hair comb aside to allow the glue to dry fully before using.

When working with glue, protect your work surface with newspaper or a cover of some sort.

Making the woven button fascinator

Thread a tapestry needle with yarn, using a different colour for each of the four buttons. To cover the plastic creative button base, bring the needle up through the centre of the button, then over and under the plastic mesh, bringing the needle back out at the centre to complete the first wrapping of the yarn. Repeat this wrapping process but this time bring the needle up through the middle section instead of the centre (Fig. 1).

To avoid getting into a tangle, it is better to work with a few shorter lengths of yarn

rather than one longer length of thread – 35–40cm/14–16in is a good length.

Continue the wrapping technique, wrapping from the centre and the middle sections, until the button is completely covered.

Fig 1

If you worked every wrap through the centre, the yarn would not lie flat.

Secure the yarn by working a few stitches on the wrong side of the button base. Work backstitch circles with white embroidery thread by working in and out of the gaps left where the yarn was wrapped from the middle sections.

When stitching the buttons together, you could pop a bead or two onto the thread to make a beaded cluster at the centre.

Attach the completed buttons to the comb. With the front of the comb facing you, place the first button in position in between the legs of the comb; turn the comb over and thread the cord elastic through the button shank (Fig. 2). Repeat this process until all the buttons are in place. With the front of the comb facing you once again, bring the elastic to the front around the outer legs and knot the ends together, making sure the elastic is pulled tight and that it is secure. Trim off the excess and allow the knot to sit hidden behind the buttons.

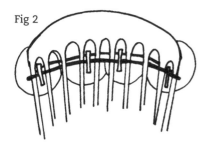

Fig 2

Make sure the comb you choose has sufficient space between its legs to accommodate the shanks of the moulded plastic buttons.

DESIGN INSPIRATIONS

Ditch your bought buttons and raid your granny's button collection for that retro vibe.

•

For extra novelty value, decorate the large background buttons with cute animal-shaped buttons.

•

To give your woven buttons extra sparkle, use metallic embroidery threads for the backstitch and add a few bead accents.

•

Play about with the size of buttons used – try different combinations or go for a super stack of three or more.

BEADED BEAUTY

What better way to add a sparkle to your day than with this beaded hair comb? I have used a mixture of freshwater pearls, droplet-style glass beads and bugles in complementary colours for the eye-catching embellishment, but you can make yours using any beads you have available.

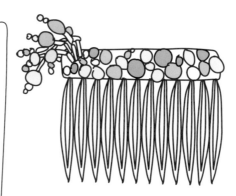

Materials

- Hair comb
- 0.4mm silver-plated copper craft wire
- Selection of beads: glass beads and freshwater pearls in assorted sizes, and small bugles

Preparing for work

It is a good idea to set out all the different beads in little piles on your work surface – saucers work well for this. Next cut a length of wire approx. 30cm (12in).

Covering the comb top

Working from right to left, wrap the end of the wire around the top of the comb to secure into position. Using the glass and pearl beads, place your first bead onto the wire and, making sure that the bead is sitting to the top, wrap the wire around the comb to keep it in place. Repeat this process, alternating the size and colour of the beads as you go. Continue wrapping the wire and placing beads randomly until most of the top of the comb is covered, stopping approx. 2cm (¾in) from the end ready to add the bead spray decoration (Fig. 1).

Fig 1

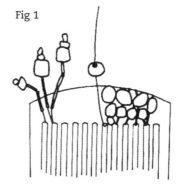

You do not need to work out the bead design in advance – just as long as your bead colours tone together, it will be fine.

Making the bead spray decoration

Cut a length of wire approx. 30cm (12in), thread on a small glass bead and place at the centre of the wire. Fold the wire in half and gently twirl the bead with your fingers to twist the wire and secure the position of the bead. Next take a larger glass bead and thread both ends of the wire through it; repeat with a pearl; then slip on about three or four bugle beads to complete the bead strand. Make seven bead strands in all, four long and three short.

Gather up the longer bead strands and twist the wires together; wrap the wire twist around the gap left at the left-hand side of the comb and spread out to form the back of the spray.

If necessary, wrap a piece of wire around the longer bead strands to secure them in position.

Take the three shorter beaded strands and attach individually by wrapping into position in between the longer sections already attached. You can add as a group if you prefer, but attaching one at a time will give you more flexibility with the placement.

Continue to wrap beads as before to cover up any gaps left where you have attached the bead spray decoration.

Finishing off

To make sure there are no loose ends of wire poking out that may get caught in the hair, gently run your finger along the back of the comb to feel for sharp edges. If you find any, press them flat with round-nose pliers, but be careful not to crush any of the beads.

DESIGN INSPIRATIONS

Try using a different type of hair comb for the base – metal or tortoiseshell perhaps – and choose the colour palette of your beads accordingly.

•

You could attach a bead spray decoration to a comb that already has the top bar decorated, and see if you can blend in the two styles.

•

Be inventive with the mix of beads you use, but be careful not to use too heavy a bead for the top of the spray decoration as it might start to droop.

•

Have a rummage about in your jewellery box for any odd earrings or unwanted costume jewellery to utilize in your design.

VINTAGE FEATHERS

Finding authentic vintage-style feathers can be expensive, but you can make your own from bits 'n' bobs, and with the addition of a little hand-stitched embroidery the finished piece will look absolutely stunning.

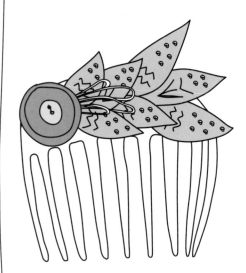

Materials

- Hair comb
- Felt fabric: black and beige
- Embroidery threads: cream, gold, orange and bronze
- Thin space-dyed cord, approx. 1m (39¼in)
- Buttons: one large, one small

Making the feather base

Using the 6cm (2⅜in) leaf/feather template as a guide (see Templates), cut eight feathers from the black felt. Referring to Fig. 1, work the embroidery to add the feather pattern. Working with two strands of thread in your needle, embroider each petal with French knots (top), straight stitch zigzags (middle) and fly stitch (base), varying the colour thread used (see Techniques for more advice on working the stitches).

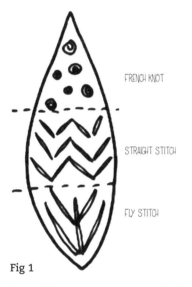

FRENCH KNOT

STRAIGHT STITCH

FLY STITCH

Fig 1

As real feathers are never exactly the same, you don't have to worry about getting yours to match – it will add to the effect if they are all slightly different.

Next use the tearbrop base template (see Templates) to cut out a base from the beige felt. Attach the feathers to the base using Fig. 2 as a guide to positioning; pin then stitch to secure.

Fig 2

Adding the loop embellishment

Cut the space-dyed cord into four equal pieces. Take one piece and fold it in half; tie a knot to make a loop approx. 6cm (2⅜in) at the top. Repeat for the other three pieces. Using Fig. 3 as a guide, pin and stitch the loops onto the feathers.

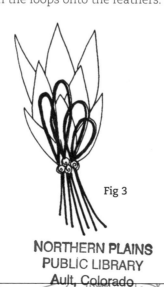

Fig 3

NORTHERN PLAINS
PUBLIC LIBRARY
Ault, Colorado

You don't need to be to exact when making the loops – a slight variation in size will add to the effect.

Place the smaller button on top of the larger button and stitch together. Place the button stack onto the feather base, making sure that it covers the knots of the decorative loops.

Attaching the feather decoration to the comb

Place the feather embellishment onto the comb, and play about with how it is sitting until you are completely happy that you have the angle right. Using a sharp needle and a strong sewing cotton, carefully stitch the base to the comb by working the thread around the top of the comb and in between the legs. Trim back the cord tails as necessary to finish.

To avoid flattening the finished felt feathers, work the attaching stitches at the very base of them.

DESIGN INSPIRATIONS
You could use beads instead of embroidery stitches to create the feather pattern.

•

As an alternative to cord, try using leather thong or a fine satin ribbon for the loop embellishment.

OVERSIZED FLOWER

This beautiful, bold fascinator is great for those special occasions. I have made two versions to inspire you to create your own.

Materials

For the fabric flower
- Two 20cm (8in) squares of four complementary printed fabrics
- 50cm (20in) fusible webbing
- 12cm (4¾in) square of felt fabric
- Hair comb
- Embroidery threads
- Selection of beads: seed, size 6 and 8, bugle and lozenge
- 0.2mm silver-plated craft wire

For the felt flower
- 20cm (8in) squares of four felts in the same shade range
- 12cm (4¾in) square of felt fabric
- Hair comb
- Glass seed beads size 6
- Small quantity of feathers

Preparing and cutting fabric

For the fabric flower
Iron your chosen fabric to remove any creases before marking and cutting. You will need a total of eight circles of fabric, two of each size, approx. 9cm (3½in), 11cm (4¼in), 15cm (5⅝in) and 20cm (8in). Fusible webbing is used to join the cut fabric together to give you four reversible circles. You can choose to cut same-size circles from matching fabric prints or from differing fabric prints, as you prefer.

Mark the circle outline on the wrong side of the fabric and carefully cut out around it. For each circle size, cut two from printed fabric and one from fusible webbing. Place the rough side of the fusible webbing circle onto the wrong side of one of the fabric circles, making sure that they match exactly; press with a hot iron. Allow the fabric to cool and remove the backing. Place the second fabric circle wrong side down onto the fusible webbing, checking that the edges match; press with a hot iron to fix.

For the felt flower
Cut a 9cm (3½in), 11cm (4¼in), 15cm (5⅝in) and 20cm (8in) circle – one only – from each 20cm (8in) square of felt.

Creating the petals

Take a fabric/felt circle and fold in half, then in half again (Fig. 1). Using a ballpoint pen draw a heart shape or a wavy line along the top edge.

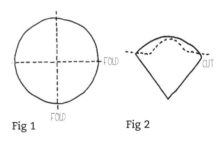

Fig 1   Fig 2

Using a sharp pair of scissors, cut to the inside of the line so that the pen mark is removed (Fig. 2); open out to reveal the petals. Repeat for all the circles.

Try experimenting on a piece of paper first to create different petal shapes.

Embellishing the petals

For the fabric flower
Let the pattern of the printed fabrics you have chosen guide you when embellishing the petals, and work decorative stitches with two strands of embroidery thread to highlight selected motifs (see Techniques). Other ideas include working lines of running stitch to emphasize the shape of the petals or stitching a random scattering of French knots (or beads) across the petal (Fig. 3).

For the felt flower
Stitch the glass seed beads around the outer edge of the largest petal circle using sewing thread.

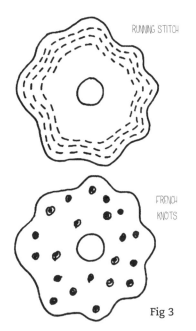

RUNNING STITCH

FRENCH KNOTS

Fig 3

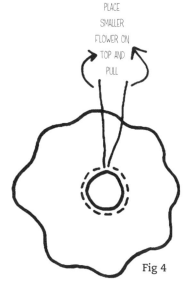

PLACE SMALLER FLOWER ON TOP AND PULL

Fig 4

For design inspirations to change the look of your fascinator, see overleaf.

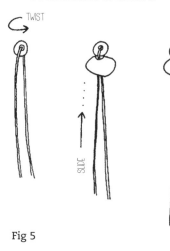

TWIST

SLIDE

Fig 5

through a sharp sewing needle, insert down through the centre of the flower and out at the back. Pull tight to ensure that the beads are sitting above one another with no gaps in between, and work a few backstitches to secure.

Putting the petals together

Put the smaller 9cm (3½in) petal to one side. Fold each of the remaining petals in turn into quarters, folding in half, then in half again; snip off the bottom pointed section so that when you open out the petal there will be a hole in the middle.

Now fold the 9cm (3½in) petal into quarters and pinch together at the fold to form a flower; pin, then hand-stitch to secure.

Take the 11cm (4¼in) petal and work a running stitch around the centre hole approx. 5mm (¼in) in from the edge (Fig. 4). Place the 9cm (3½in) flower into the hole and pull the thread tight to gather up the petals. Pin and stitch into position. Repeat until all the petal layers are attached to each other, ascending in size.

Making the beaded centre

For the fabric flower only
Referring to Fig. 5 and the following instructions, make seven stamens.

Cut a 50cm (20in) length of craft wire. Thread a small seed bead onto the wire and position at the centre. Fold the wire in half and gently twirl the bead with your fingers several times – this will twist the wire and secure the bead's position.

Thread both ends of the wire through the large seed bead and slide up to meet the small seed bead. Continue to add the lozenge bead and several bugle beads, varying the number of bugle beads used to make the stamen longer or shorter.

To attach the stamen to the fabric flower, thread the wire ends

Finishing off

Cut a 10cm (4in) circle from the small felt fabric square. Place the hair comb in the centre and stitch in place – the comb needs to be able to move, so while it needs to be securely stitched, it must remain flexible.

Pin the felt circle onto the underside of the flower. Place the fascinator onto your head to check that you are happy with how it is sitting. Make any necessary adjustments before stitching the comb base in place.

For the felt flower only
Arrange a tuft of feathers to one side of the largest petal. Feathers are available from most good haberdasheries.

BAND OF BUTTONS

All you need to make the perfect stay-put, non-slip multiband are three narrow headbands, an oddment of cotton fabric long enough to cover the length of the bands, a few scraps of colourful felt and some buttons.

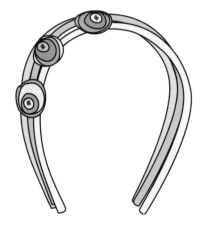

Materials

- Three fine headbands approx. 5mm (¼in) wide
- Two sheets of black felt fabric approx. 23 x 30.5cm (9 x 12in)
- 42 x 15cm (16½ x 6in) cotton fabric
- 42 x 15cm (16½ x 6in) fusible webbing
- 42 x 15cm (16½ x 6in) interfacing
- Felt in several different colours
- Three buttons approx. 1.5cm (⅝in)
- Two elastic bands

Preparing the headbands

Cover the headbands with the black felt fabric following the instructions for a Simple Covered Headband (see Techniques). Then use the cotton fabric to cover them again, following the instructions for a Fabric Covered Headband.

Joining the headbands

Gather up the covered bands and wrap an elastic band around each end of the headband bundle. Play about with how the bands are sitting, and place them on your head to make sure that they are spaced out evenly. Make any necessary adjustments and, once you are happy, pin together to secure.

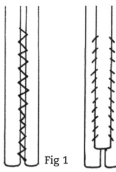

Fig 1   Fig 2

Now stitch the bands together; move the elastic band further up out of the way, and, with the legs still gathered, sew securely. You may find it easier to place two bands side by side and sew together first (Fig. 1), before going on to place and stitch the third band in between the first two bands (Fig. 2).

Making the felt button decorations

For each felt button decoration, cut three circles from felt fabric in the following sizes: 4cm (1½in), 3.5cm (1⅜in) and 2.5cm (1in). Use a mix of different colours.

Sew a button onto the smallest felt circle, then layer this up onto the 3.5cm (1⅜in) felt circle, and again onto the 4cm (1½in) felt circle. Stitch the layered felt circles together using backstitch or running stitch. Make three layered felt button stacks in all.

Pin the finished felt button decorations onto the multiband. Check in the mirror that you like where they are sitting. Once you are happy with the placement, sew on the felt button decorations securely, working from the underside of the design and using a thread colour to tone in with the fabric so that the stitches won't be seen – use a hem stitch and sew the bottom layer of the felt to the band on its outer edges.

> ### DESIGN INSPIRATIONS
> *Use a different patterned fabric to cover each headband.*
>
> •
>
> *Decorate the multiband with reclaimed jewellery embellishments and use a clear-drying fabric glue to stick them on.*
>
> •
>
> *Why stop at three layers? See how many more you can add.*

FLAPPER STYLE

Small leaf-shapes are cut out from felt and stitched together, and embellished with real feathers, buttons and beads, to create these flapper-style decorations. Two variations are provided, but as felt fabric is available in a rainbow of colours you can create your own colour combinations.

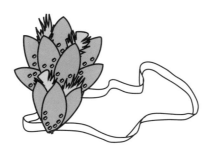

Materials
For the bright design
- Felt fabric: two shades of green and three shades yellow (for the feathers); beige (for the base); purple, brown and turquoise (for the loop detail)
- Creative button (see Suppliers)
- Turquoise embroidery thread
- Eight multi-coloured glass beads, assorted sizes
- 15cm (6in) feather
- 9mm wide black elastic, approx. 60cm (24in) long

For the black design
- Black felt fabric
- Feathers: four green and three turquoise
- 15 clear glass beads, size 8
- 9mm wide black elastic, approx. 60cm (24in) long

Cutting and preparing the felt

Using the leaf/feather templates (see Templates) as a guide to shape, cut your felt fabric for your chosen design as outlined below.

For the bright design
Feathers
Three bright green 4 x 2cm (1½ x ¾in) (A).
Three lime green 3 x 1.5cm (1⅛ x ⅝in) (B).
Five bright yellow 6 x 2.5cm (2⅜ x 1in) (C).
Four gold 4 x 2cm (1½ x ¾in) (D).
Three pale yellow 4 x 2cm (1½ x ¾in) (E).
Loops
Cut 20cm (8in) lengths approx. 5mm (¼in) wide: two purple; two turquoise; three brown.
Base
Cut one teardrop base from the beige felt fabric (see Templates).

For the black design
Cut eight feathers 4 x 2cm (1½ x ¾in) and one teardrop base from the black felt fabric.

Note, the sizes given for the feathers are approximate and each shape does not need to be exact.

Constructing the feather design

Set out all the pieces you will be using for your chosen design.

For the bright design
Referring to Fig. 1 and to the photograph to guide you, pin the felt shapes and loops onto the beige felt base, and stitch in place using matching or tonal threads.

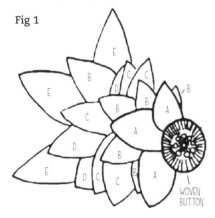

Fig 1

Next make the woven button. Thread a tapestry needle with the turquoise embroidery thread. Bring the needle up through the centre of the button, then over and under the plastic mesh, bringing the needle back out at the centre to complete the first wrapping of the yarn. Repeat this wrapping process but this time bring the needle up through the middle section instead of the centre. Continue the wrapping technique, wrapping from the centre and the middle sections, until the button is completely covered. Secure the thread at the back.

To embellish the woven button, stitch on a circle of glass beads. Place the completed button at the centre of the front three felt feathers and stitch to the base. Stitch the 15cm (6in) feather in position on the underside of the base.

For the black design
Referring to Fig. 2 and to the photograph to guide you, pin the felt shapes and the green and turquoise feathers onto the black felt base, and stitch in place using matching or tonal threads.

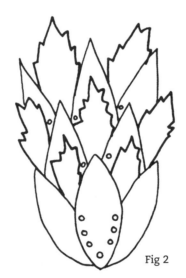

Fig 2

Sew seven of the clear glass beads onto the centre front felt feather, then randomly stitch the remaining beads in between the felt shapes and the feathers.

Making the elastic headband

Measure the elastic around your head – make sure it is stretched slightly and that it feels comfortable and not too tight. Fold the ends over each other by approx. 1.5cm (⅝in); pin and then stitch.

When joining the elastic ends your sewing doesn't need to be perfect as it will be covered by the flapper decoration.

Finishing off

Pin the completed feather decoration onto the elastic headband so that it covers the join. Make sure you are happy with how it is sitting; check in a mirror and make any necessary adjustments before stitching the decoration in place on the band.

DESIGN INSPIRATIONS
Substitute the feathers for other felt motifs – simple shapes work best, such as a heart or diamond.

•

Create your own colour scheme. Looking for some inspiration? Mother Nature has put together some fantastic combinations in flowers.

•

Use embroidery or beaded embellishments to decorate the felt motifs.

TAKE A BOW

Take a simple shop-bought band and use three different widths of tartan ribbon to cover it and make the beautiful bow.

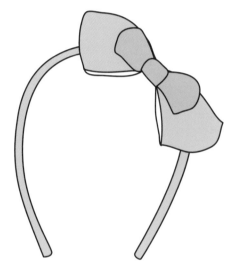

Preparing the headband

Cover the headband with the black felt fabric following the instructions for a Simple Covered Headband (see Techniques). Then use the longer length of 5cm (2in) wide tartan ribbon to cover again, following the instructions for a Fabric Covered Headband.

Making the bow

Fold in the ends of the 7cm (2¾in) wide tartan ribbon to create a loop at both sides, and overlap the ends where they meet in the middle; pin (Fig. 1).

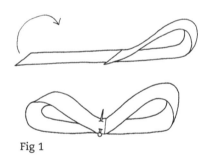

Fig 1

Ribbon with wired edges works well for the bow.

Using a running stitch, sew through all the layers at the centre seam; pull the thread to ruck up the ribbon slightly (Fig. 2). Work a backstitch to secure the rucking. Repeat to make a smaller bow from the remaining length of 5cm (2in) wide ribbon.

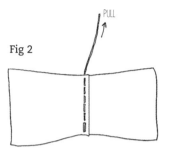

PULL

Fig 2

Place the small bow on top of the large bow, matching up the centre seams; pin if necessary. Wrap the 2cm (¾in) wide ribbon around the centre of the bows a couple of times (Fig. 3). Cut the ribbon a couple of centimetres (about an inch) from the end; fold under and hand-stitch to secure.

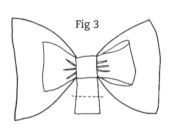

Fig 3

Finishing off

Place the tartan bow slightly off centre on the covered headband, and stitch in place. Sew in all loose thread ends.

This headband is perfect for a college preppy look or a street pop punk vibe. For great styling ideas, see the design inspirations overleaf.

Materials

- Headband approx. 1cm (⅜in) wide
- Black felt fabric to cover headband
- 2cm (¾in) wide tartan ribbon, approx. 10cm (4in) long
- 5cm (2in) wide tartan ribbon, two lengths approx. 42cm (16½in) and 20cm (8in) long
- 7cm (2¾in) wide tartan ribbon, approx. 35cm (13¾in) long

TRIO OF ROSES

In this project I've used reclaimed fabric and buttons for the rolled rose flowers. Searching through my wardrobe for garments that were past their best, an old spotty T-shirt, stripy shirt and fine-gauge knitted cotton jumper gave me this classic and ever-popular red, white and blue combination.

Materials

- Fine headband approx. 5mm (¼in) wide
- Black felt fabric to cover headband
- Three 13cm (5in) wide fabric strips at least 50cm (20in) long
- Three buttons to match your fabric choice

Preparing the headband

Cover the headband with the black felt fabric following the instructions for a Simple Covered Headband (see Techniques).

Making the basic rolled flower

Take one of your chosen fabric strips, fold over the long edges by 1cm (⅜in) and press with a steam iron to fix the folds in place. Fold over the folded edges by 1cm (⅜in) to create a hem; press.

Bring hem edges together and press lengthways. If the fabric is cotton/polycotton and has been pressed with a steam iron, the strip will keep its shape and shouldn't open out. If necessary – if you are using a silky fabric for example – you can sew the edges together by machine or by hand.

Fold the strip at its centre to form a right angle (Fig. 1). Continue folding one side over the other until the length has been used up (Fig. 2).

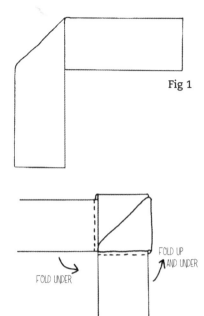

Fig 1

Fig 2

FOLD UNDER

FOLD UP AND UNDER

Hold the ends of the strip together letting the folded part fall away. Hold the ends lightly in between your left-hand finger and thumb, and use your right-hand to smoothly and gently pull one of the lengths. The fabric will gather up to create a flower shape. Pin the base to secure the shape, and stitch using a sharp sewing needle and a thread to match the fabric. Sew a button in the centre of the flower.

Choose your buttons once the flowers have been made as the look of the fabric can change dramatically.

Finishing off

Once all three roses have been completed, place slightly off centre into position on the headband one at a time. Working from the underside of the flowers, stitch them to the band making sure that you sew both through the base of the flowers and the felt fabric.

Use a thread shade that tones in with the felt colour you have used for covering the headband – it's best to go for a slightly darker shade if an exact match is not available.

DESIGN INSPIRATIONS

Play about with the placement of the flowers to create a different look.

•

Work beads or sequins in the flower centres instead of a button for a sparkly finish.

•

Discover how different widths of fabric strips make different size flowers.

•

Substitute ribbon for the fabric strips, approx. 6–7cm (2⅜–2¾in) wide as hemming is not required; if using shiny ribbon, take care as it can slip about when making the flower.

NAUTICAL CHIC

These decorated headbands have a touch of the military or naval dress uniform about them. Both are based on using fancy shop-bought frog fasteners for the decoration, although the silver design also uses knitted I-cord which you can make yourself.

Ornate frog fasteners are the secret to pulling off this uniform look. The look of your design will depend on the type you buy and most good haberdashery shops will have a selection to choose from.

Materials

For the gold design

- Fine headband approx. 5mm (¼in) wide
- Sheet of black felt fabric approx. 23 x 30.5cm (9 x 12in)
- One metallic gold frog fastener, approx. 9 x 1.5cm (3½ x ⅝in) (see Suppliers)

For the silver design

- Fine headband approx. 5mm (¼in) wide
- Sheet of black felt fabric approx. 23 x 30.5cm (9 x 12in)
- Silver-grey 4ply (fine-weight) yarn
- Two 3mm (size 2) double-pointed knitting needles
- Two metallic silver (three-loop) frog fasteners, approx. 5 x 2.5cm (2 x 1in)

Making the gold headband

Cover the headband with black felt fabric following the instructions for a Simple Covered Headband (see Techniques). Cut two lozenge bases from the leftovers (see Templates).

Pin and stitch the gold frog fastener onto one of the felt lozenge bases. Layer the second felt lozenge piece over the back to cover the stitching and to make the felt fabric base stiffer; pin and stitch together by working a running stitch approx. 5mm (¼in) in from the outer edge.

Stitch the decoration onto the covered headband, slightly off centre, using a black thread so that the stitches will not show.

Making the silver headband

Cover the headband with black felt fabric following the instructions for a Simple Covered Headband (see Techniques). Cut two oval bases from the leftovers (see Templates).

Make 40cm (15½in) of knitted I-cord from the silver-grey 4ply (fine-weight) yarn. Use the knitted I-cord to make a four-loop design (Fig. 1); pin and stitch the loops where they cross over to ensure the design keeps its shape, and make sure that you join the design ends together on the underside.

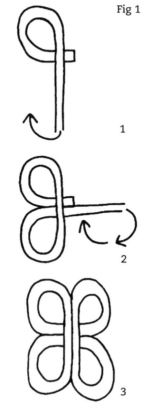

Fig 1

1

2

3

As an alternative to the knitted I-cord, you could use 1cm (⅜in) wide silver cord to make the loop embellishment.

Referring to the photograph of the finished project, pin the loop embellishment to the centre of one of the felt oval bases. Place a silver frog fastener to either side of it, so that the section with the knot sits at the outer edge of the oval and the other loop section sits snugly in between the loops of the loop embellishment. Sew in place. Layer the second felt oval piece over the back to cover the stitching and to make the felt fabric base stiffer; pin and stitch together by working a running stitch approx. 5mm (¼in) in from the outer edge.

Stitch the finished decoration onto the covered headband, slightly off centre, using a black thread so that the stitches will not show on the black felt.

Making knitted I-cord

An I-cord is basically a knitted tube. Make as follows:

Using 3mm (size 2) double-pointed knitting needles, cast on 4 stitches. Hold the needle with the stitches in your left hand and make sure the length of yarn attached to the ball is on the left-hand side of the work.

Next slide the stitches up to the right-hand tip of the needle and knit to the end – do not turn the needle, simply slide the stitches back up to the right-hand tip of the left-hand needle and knit to the end.

Continue to knit in this way until you have the length of cord required, then cast off.

To make your own loop design, take a length of string and twist up into your preferred shape (Fig. 2); trim and measure to determine the length of I-cord that you need to knit.

Fig 2

DESIGN INSPIRATIONS

Experiment with different types of cord or even ribbon to make your own frog fasteners.

•

Play about to create your own loop embellishment design.

•

Add beads and buttons to the finished motif for extra decoration.

•

Celtic knots and cable designs can provide great inspiration when working on your own knitted I-cord design.

•

Unsure of the length of I–cord needed? It's best to make a longer length and not to cast off, as you can always unravel back to the length required.

GLITTERY GLAMOUR

A random pattern of glass and pearl beads are wired onto a circle base to create this lovely clip, and just as long as your beads tone in together, the design will work out just fine.

Materials

- Sectioning hair clip 9cm (3½in) long
- 1.2mm sterling-plated craft wire
- 0.4mm silver-plated copper craft wire
- 0.2mm silver-plated copper craft wire
- Selection of glass and pearl beads, size 4, 6 and 8, in complementary colours
- Round-nose pliers
- Cork stopper

Making the base circle

Cut a 60cm (23½in) length of 1.2mm wire. Form into a circle approx. 8cm (3⅛in) in diameter and several layers thick. Twist the ends of the wire around the circle to secure.

Cut 30cm (12in) lengths of 0.4mm wire and wrap around the wire circle to cover the original wire completely. (Note, using smaller lengths makes it easier to wrap the wire around the circle; when joining in a new piece of wire, use the pliers to flatten the ends.)

Make the wire circle about 5mm (¼in) shorter than the sectioning clip at each end so that it can be attached comfortably.

Attaching the base circle onto the clip

Place the circle on the clip and use another length of 0.4mm wire in a figure-of-eight motion to attach it; wrap the ends around the circle and flatten with the pliers.

Open up the clip and place the cork stopper in between to keep it open. Wrap 0.4mm wire around what has now become the centre bar of the clip, until it is completely covered. Carefully run your finger over the underside to feel for sharp edges – if you find any, press them flat with the pliers.

As the whole clip will be covered with beads, don't worry about being too neat when covering with wire.

Decorating with beads

Cut 30cm (12in) lengths of 0.2mm wire. Wrap the end of the first length of wire around the outer circle to secure into position. Place a bead onto the wire and, making sure that the bead is sitting to the top, wrap the wire around the circle, then around the bead to keep it in place. Repeat until the outer circle has been covered, alternating the beads used to give a random effect.

Now move on to cover the centre bar with wired-on beads in the same way, remembering to use the cork stopper in between the legs to keep the clip open.

If you find that there are any gaps appearing on the covered clip, simply repeat the wrapping process adding small seed beads into the gaps.

Set out all the different beads in little piles on your work surface – saucers work well for this.

Finishing off

Once again, carefully run your finger over the underside to feel for sharp edges – if you find any, press them flat with the pliers taking care not to squash or crush the beads. To make quite sure that no sharp wire edges will poke into the head or get caught in the hair, use a glue gun to apply a line of adhesive along the underside of the centre bar and the outer circle. If you don't have a glue gun, use superglue. Use a cork stopper to keep the centre bar clip open until the glue is completely dry.

DESIGN INSPIRATIONS

To make a smaller version of the Glittery Glamour hair clip, just use a smaller clip.

•

For a unique look, experiment with different types of beads. Source costume jewellery or beaded necklaces from charity shops and thrift stores – you will be amazed at what you can find.

•

Try using a different shape for the wire base – a geometric shape such as a square or a diamond, or a heart shape, would work well.

•

Why limit yourself to silver wire when there are so many gorgeous colours of craft wire available?

•

Choose beads from complementary shades and mix together to give this project a whole new look.

MINIATURE ROSES

This delicately simple yet beautiful interpretation of a flower is made from a folded fabric strip, but the secret to its realistic shape is the placing of a piece of piping cord trapped along the folded edge with a running stitch.

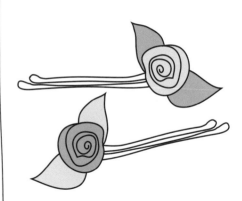

Materials (for each flower)

- 15 x 5cm (6 x 2in) of cotton fabric
- 3mm (⅛in) piping cord, approx. 20cm (8in)
- 10cm (4in) square of green felt fabric
- Kirby grips

Preparing the fabric

Iron your chosen cotton fabric to remove any creases. Fold the fabric in half lengthways and press to form a crease. Open out the fabric and place the piping cord along the crease (Fig. 1); carefully fold the fabric back in half and pin together just beneath where the cord is sitting on the crease.

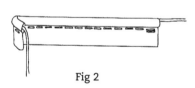

CORD   **Fig 1**   FOLD

Thread a sharp sewing needle with sewing cotton to match and work a line of running stitch beneath the piping cord (Fig. 2).

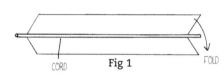

Fig 2

When the fabric is rolled up to make the flower shape, the cord leaves a lovely defined and rounded top edge.

Making the rolled flower

Fold the edge of the fabric strip inwards so that piping cord is vertical (Fig. 2), then tightly roll the rest of the fabric around the piping cord, folding the end of the strip inwards to finish. Pin to secure the rolled up flower so it keeps its shape.

Taking your needle, secure the sewing thread to the fabric and work a couple of stitches at the outer edge fold, then insert the needle straight through the roll. Keep working straight through the base of the roll, working your way around, inserting the needle through all the layers (Fig. 3).

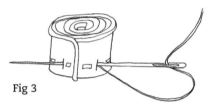

Fig 3

Next work a running stitch around the outside edge and pull tight to gather in the base of the rose. Work a couple of backstitches to secure.

Making the felt leaves

Make two or three leaves to decorate (see Ribbon Rose Garland), and pin in position so that they cover the base of the rolled flower. Stitch in place, and leave your needle threaded to attach the flower to the grip.

Attaching the flower to the grip

Bring the thread in between the legs of the grip and up towards the top loop; bring the needle over the top of the grip and insert it into the base fabric and back out again, and in between the legs of grip, repeating until the grip is securely attached.

DESIGN INSPIRATIONS

Use a length of ribbon to create the miniature rose, but before buying do check that your ribbon choice folds in half easily – grosgrain or petersham will be too thick.

•

For added dimension, stitch a few tiny beads to the edge following the line of the piping cord.

•

Scale the rose up and attach it to a sectioning clip – just use a broader strip of fabric and a thicker piping cord.

FLOWER CUT OUTS

Choose a bold floral print and zone in on motifs that can be easily cut out. My fabric choice inspired two designs — a cluster of small, overlapping beaded flowers and a single bloom with individually cut petals.

All the shapes have been cut individually and stitched into position on a felt base; which is then stitched onto the clip so that it sits flush and follows the line of the clip.

Materials

- Floral patterned cotton fabric
- Fusible webbing
- Interfacing
- Click-clack hair clip
- Felt fabric to cover clip
- Small glass beads

Making the floral embellishment

Iron your chosen fabric to remove any creases before starting. Choose which motifs you want to use from the fabric. Cut a piece of fusible webbing and interfacing appropriate to the size of your chosen motifs. Place the rough side of the fusible webbing onto the wrong side of the fabric; press with a hot iron. Allow the fabric to cool. Remove the backing from the fusible webbing and place the interfacing onto it; press with a hot iron to fix. Once the fabric has cooled, carefully cut out the floral motif you have chosen. Note, for the single flower, I cut out two flower heads from the fabric, so that I could use one as a base and the other for layering on extra petals for a 3D effect.

Attaching the floral embellishment to a felt base

Place the clip onto the felt fabric and draw around the outline to give you your base; cut out.

If you prefer, you could make a paper template of the clip shape to ensure you are happy with the shape before using it to cut out the felt.

Start playing with the placement of your cut motifs onto the felt base – allow the small flowers to overlap each other – and once you are happy, pin and stitch them onto the felt fabric to secure in place. (For the large flower, only the stem and the centre of the petals need to be stitched to the felt base.) As the fabric has been stiffened with interfacing, the flowers/petals will keep their shape, and the fabric won't fray and unravel. Stitch some beads to the centre of the small flowers to add a bit of sparkle.

Attaching the felt base to the clip

Secure thread to the underside of the felt fabric at its narrowest end; place the felt base in position on the hair clip and either pin to secure or hold in place with your left hand. Using Fig. 1 as a guide, stitch around the bars of the clip, bringing the needle and thread over the bar into the fabric and back out towards the centre.

Make sure the colour of your sewing thread matches the colour of your felt.

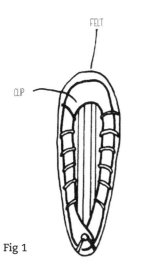

FELT

CLIP

Fig 1

DESIGN INSPIRATIONS

Hunt around in fabric stores for interesting remnants, and look in your local charity shop for retro prints and patterns.

•

Decorate the petals with embroidery stitches such as running stitch or French knots but do this before stitching them to the felt base.

•

Geometrics, abstracts and florals all work brilliantly for this style of project.

•

Cut plain or closely patterned fabrics into shapes of your own design, such as a butterfly motif or a heart shape.

COVER UP

Customize a set of self-cover buttons to use as a decorative embellishment for your hair clips. The fun begins when you choose your fabrics.

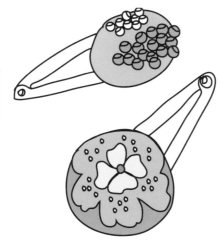

Materials (for each button set)

- Three metal self-cover buttons: 19mm, 23mm and 29mm
- Three pieces of 10cm (4in) square cotton/polycotton fabric
- Three click-clack hair clips
- Embroidery threads and selection of seed and bugle beads for embellishing
- Round-nose pliers

Choosing your fabric

You do not need a large amount of fabric to cover a button – just twice the width of the button size. Some fabrics will work better than others: if the fabric is too thick, the back of the button will not clip together; if it is too fine, the metal will shine through. A dressmaking weight is ideal, but finer fabrics can be used if doubled or backed with an interfacing.

When choosing your pattern or print, remember that the fabric size cut for each button is approximately twice the size of the finished button. To check how the pattern or print will look on the button front, cut a disc to the finished button size. A small repeat pattern will give a more uniform, all-over print, while a large pattern will look more abstract.

Covering a button

Use the pliers to pull out the metal shank from the centre of the button to remove the button back (Fig. 1).

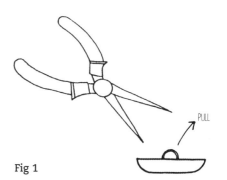

PULL

Fig 1

The reverse of the button packet often provides a guide to the size of fabric circle required to cover the button.

Cut out a circle from your chosen fabric approx. twice the size of the button to be covered. If you want to add embellishments, do so now, following the ideas given in Customizing Your Button and Design Inspirations.

Using sewing thread, work a running stitch approx. 5mm (¼in) in from the outer edge of the fabric circle, but do not finish off the thread ends. With the fabric facing right side down, place the button in the centre. Take the loose thread ends and gently pull, gathering the fabric up and around the button (Fig. 2). Tie a knot to secure.

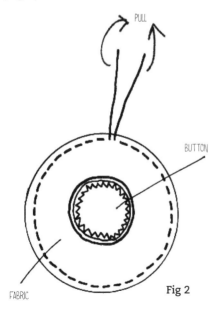

PULL

BUTTON

FABRIC

Fig 2

Making sure that the ridges are facing down the right way, click the button back in place.

Customizing your button

Use the embroidery threads and bead selection to embellish your fabric circles. I find that the fabric I have chosen dictates how I embellish: for example, lines or motifs can be followed with a running stitch; a French knot or a bead can be stitched on top of a printed dot; or, if the fabric is plain, a simple flower can be worked using daisy stitch in a contrasting colour.

Attaching the button to the clip

Add a small drop of glue to the underside of the button, taking care to stay within the centre rim to avoid getting glue on the outer edge or button front. Add a small drop of glue to the top of the clasp. Press button and clasp together, and hold tight until the glue has bonded. Set aside to allow the glue to dry fully before using.

Make sure you use a glue that is suitable for sticking metal together. A glue gun is ideal for the careful application of the adhesive.

DESIGN INSPIRATIONS

When making a set of three buttons, leave one unembellished to let the fabric print speak for itself.

•

Use beads and simple embroidery stitches to emphasize the patterns and motifs on your chosen fabrics.

•

Use a simple embroidered motif or part of an iron-on transfer to decorate plain fabrics.

•

Try making your own fabric – cut strips of suitable fabrics and sew them together to make stripes.

•

When stitching your fabric strips together, machine zigzag stitch works particularly well.

•

To embellish buttons that have already been covered, it is easiest to glue on the embellishments rather than stitch them on, using a suitable adhesive (always check the product instructions).

PRETTY KNITTY FLOWERS

With only the most basic knit or crochet skills, you can quickly transform a few scraps of yarn and a selection of beads into a great set of cute floral hair grips. Simply mix and match these knit and crochet delights to create your own selection of wonderful blooms.

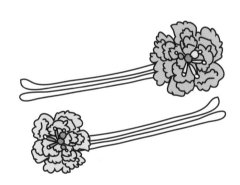

Materials

- Oddments of 4ply (fine-weight) or DK (light-weight) cotton-based yarn
- 3mm (D3) crochet hook or 3.25mm (size 3) knitting needle
- Selection of seed beads
- 0.3mm coated craft wire
- Kirby grips

Working the crochet flower

With 3mm (D3) hook and yarn colour of your choice, make 8 chain (ch) plus 1 turning ch.
Row 1 Miss 1st ch, insert hook into 2nd ch from hook, * yarn round hook (yrh) and draw through (2 loops on hook), yrh and pull through both loops on hook (1 loop on hook) – 1 double crochet (dc) has been worked. Insert hook into next ch and repeat from * to end of ch working 1 dc into each chain, turn. (8 sts)

   On the next row you will be making the petal loops by working a simple chain then attaching to the base to form a loop.
Row 2 5 ch, miss 5 ch and insert hook into 1st dc, yrh and pull through, then pull through loop on hook – 1 slip stitch (ss) has been worked. Next work 5 ch then work ss into the same dc as before, next *5 ch, 1 ss into next dc, 5 ch, 1 ss into same dc, repeat from * to end.

   Break off yarn and pull through loop to secure.

Making up the crochet flower

Sew in the finishing loose end but leave the starting loose end as you will be using this to sew up the flower later. Roll up the base of the flower, so that it looks like a Swiss roll, allowing the petal loops to open out; insert a glass-headed pin through the rolled up flower base to secure.

   Next thread the remaining loose end and insert the needle through all the layers of the rolled up base; pull tight. Repeat this process a few times until the base is secure; work a few backstitches, and then snip off the yarn end.

Working the knitted flower

With 3.25mm (size 3) needles and yarn colour of your choice, cast on 42 sts.
Row 1 Knit to end.
Row 2 *K1, slip the stitch just worked back onto the left-hand needle, and then pass the 5 sts sitting behind this first stitch over and off the needle; re-knit the first stitch. Repeat from * to end. (7 sts). Break off the yarn leaving a good length for making up.

Making up the knitted flower

Thread the yarn you have just broken off through a sewing needle, and then run the sewing needle through the centre of the 7 stitches still on the knitting needle and slip the stitches off the knitting needle. Pull the yarn tight to allow the flower to roll up.

At this point, you may need to tweak the shape of the knitted flower to get the best possible result.

   Turn the flower over and insert the sewing needle up through all the layers a few times to secure. To finish, thread the loose end from the cast on edge and insert the needle down through the centre of the flower to bring it out through the back of the flower; pull tight and work a few backstitches to secure.

Basic beading for the flower centre

Cut a length of wire approx. 30cm (12in), thread on a small seed bead and place at the centre of the wire. Fold the wire in half and gently twirl the bead with your fingers a few times – this will twist the wire and secure the position of the bead. Take a larger seed bead and thread both ends of the wire through it. Thread the wire ends through a sharp sewing needle, and insert the needle down through the centre of the flower and out at the back. Pull tight to ensure that the beads are sitting above one another with no gaps in between. Work a few backstitches to secure.

Attaching the flower to the grip

Thread the needle under the bend at the top of the grip (Fig.1). Insert the needle into the base of the flower and back out under the bend of the grip. Keep wrapping the wire around the top of the grip and through the base of the flower in this way until it is secure, and finish by working a few backstitches; cut off the excess wire.

Varying the flower centre embellishment

As well as the basic beaded centre, you can use other bead combinations to vary the look. For a larger beaded centre simply slip the bead of your choice onto the wire after the large seed bead. Or, add a stamen-like embellishment to the centre of the flower by adding 3–5 bugle beads. (Note, these variations may require a longer length of wire.) If you prefer you could substitute a button for the beaded centre.

For an alternative centre decoration, make a simple beaded cluster or loop: secure the wire at the back of the flower, bring the needle up through the centre, then thread the beads on to the wire, and bring the needle to the back of the flower.

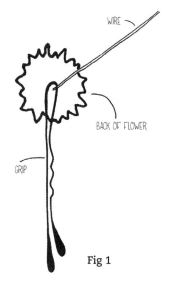

WIRE

BACK OF FLOWER

GRIP

Fig 1

If you find the flower head slips around the curve of the grip, you can add a spot of glue at the back of the flower.

PAISLEY PANACHE

This project was inspired by the traditional paisley pattern shawl. The clip design is created by layering up contrasting colours, and the addition of beads, sequins and fancy trims echo the distinctive shape and complement the colours of the fabrics.

The patterned fabric is framed by a solid colour of felt fabric, which allows the paisley shape to be seen clearly.

Materials

- 10cm (4in) square of patterned cotton fabric
- 10cm (4in) square of fusible webbing
- 10cm (4in) square of interfacing
- Felt fabric: three different colours
- 33 flat sequins
- Seed beads: size 6 and 8
- Eight bugle beads
- 5mm (¼in) wide gold ric rac, approx. 50cm (20in) long
- Sectioning hair clip 9cm (3½in) long

Preparing the fabrics

Iron the patterned cotton fabric to remove any creases. Place the rough side of the fusible webbing square onto the wrong side of the patterned cotton fabric, and press with a hot iron. Allow the fabric to cool.

Remove the backing from the fusible webbing and place the interfacing square onto it; press with a hot iron to fix. Once again, allow the fabric to cool.

Cutting fabrics

You need to make card templates of the three sections of the paisley motif – the inner, the middle and the outer sections (see Templates).

Using the outer template, cut two paisley motifs from different coloured felts. (These will be joined later to make the underside and the top side of the base.) Using the middle template, mark the outline

onto the wrong side of the fabric and cut out. Using the inner template, cut one from the remaining felt colour.

Make sure all the paisley motifs are facing in the same direction before you cut them out.

Embellishing the inner paisley motif

Place the inner felt paisley onto the middle patterned paisley, and pin. Stitch together close to the edge of the felt motif using a running stitch or backstitch.

Using the photograph as a guide, sew a line of sequins and small seed beads to hide the joining stitches. Secure the thread to the wrong side of the fabric and bring the needle up through to the right side at the lower curved edge. Place the sequin onto the needle and slide it down so that it sits flat on the fabric; next place the small seed bead onto the needle and slide it down to sit at the centre of the sequin. Take the needle back down through the centre of the sequin only, so that the small seed bead sits to the top to hold the sequin in place, and bring the needle back out to the right side of the fabric at the edge of the sequin. Repeat all around the outer edge of the felt, overlapping the sequins as you go.

Finally, work the bugle bead starburst in the centre of the motif. Secure the thread on the underside, then bring the needle up to the right side exactly where you want the centre of the pattern to be. Sew on four beads to make an 'X' shape (Fig. 1), then stitch a bead in between each leg of the 'X' to form the starburst.

Fig 1

Making up and finishing

Pin and stitch the embellished paisley layers onto one of the felt fabric bases, deciding on the felt colour that you want to be seen. Pin the ric rac so that it covers the edge of the patterned fabric and attach it with a small running stitch. Sew the larger seed beads evenly around the edge.

Next, take the remaining felt fabric base and sew the clip into position on its underside.

Check that you have the remaining base going in the same direction as the decorated top before sewing the clip to its underside.

Once the clip is secure, bring the base and the decorated top together; pin and stitch.

DESIGN INSPIRATIONS

The ric rac trim works well as it bends around the curves of the paisley motif; try experimenting with other types of trim but do make sure your choice will curve around the narrowest part of the motif.

•

Use a fancy button instead of the bugle beads as the focal point of the design.

•

This design is full of bling but you can play it down or dress it up to suit your look.

•

Instead of working one large background paisley motif, you could use two or three of the smaller motifs and overlap to cover the clip.

BEAD MOSAICS

Different sized felt circles are layered together and the top circle is divided into sections with straight stitches. Each section is then embellished with a bead pattern like a miniature mosaic design – simple but effective.

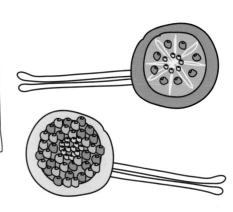

Materials

- Felt fabric: two different colours for each grip
- Embroidery thread
- Seed beads: size 6 and 8
- Kirby grips

As the name suggests this design was inspired by a mosaic – the beautifully decorated mosaic-style lids of a group of circular pots in fact.

Preparing the felt circles

For each grip, cut two circles from felt fabric approx. 4cm (1½in) and 2.5cm (1in) in diameter (you could use different-sized cotton reels to draw around). Layer the circles so that the smallest is on the top, and join together with embroidery thread, working straight stitch in a circular fashion like the spokes of a bicycle wheel (Fig. 1). Sew in the loose ends.

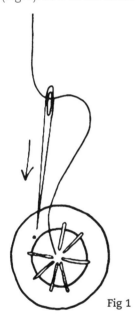

Fig 1

Adding the bead patterns

Thread a needle with a cotton sewing thread to match the colour of your beads, and secure the thread on the underside of the felt. Bring the needle out to the front of the felt circle at the narrowest point of one of the sections. Thread a bead down onto the needle, insert the needle

back through to the wrong side of the fabric, and back again into the next section. Keep working in a circular motion around the felt circle placing beads (Fig. 2). Note, you can place just one large bead in each section, or fill the sections with small beads.

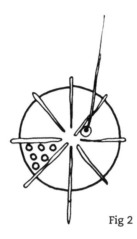

Fig 2

Finishing off

To attach the embellished felt circle to the grip, work a few backstitches on the underside of the felt. Bring the thread in between the legs of the grip and up towards the top loop; bring the needle over the top of the grip and insert it into the base fabric and back out again, and in between the legs of the grip, repeating until the grip is securely attached.

DESIGN INSPIRATIONS

Use bugle beads instead of straight stitches to define the sections of the circle and fill with French knots instead of beads.

•

Add more felt circle layers of different colours and sizes for a 3D effect.

•

Try different shapes – geometric ones work best as they aren't too fiddly to cut out.

•

Substitute a cotton fabric for the felt, but back it first with interfacing and fusible webbing to stiffen it slightly.

RIBBON ROSE GARLAND

This floral garland requires very little sewing and it really stands out with its mix of textures — shiny white roses and emerald green leaves sit on the broken sparkle of the ric rac band.

Materials

- 5mm (¼in) wide gold ric rac, approx. 160cm (63in) long
- 12 white satin ribbon roses
- Green felt and leaf-shaped glass beads (optional)

Fitting the garland

Make sure the ric rac is long enough to wrap twice around your head with enough left over to tie in a bow comfortably – a 160cm (63in) length should be fine, but it is always best to check. If you want to make a longer garland, you may need more roses.

Placing the flowers and leaves

Pin the first two roses approx. 32cm (12½in) in from each end of the ric rac band. Pin the remaining flowers randomly spaced in between. Place the garland around your head to check that you are happy with the spacing of the flowers, and adjust if necessary.

To add leaves to some of the roses, pin a leaf-shaped bead onto the band next to the flower. Cut small leaf shapes from the green felt (see Templates) and pin in place. To give the felt leaves some dimension, fold in half and stitch together a little way along the bottom curve (Fig. 1). Open out.

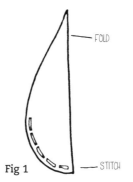

FOLD

STITCH

Fig 1

Place the garland around your head once again to check that you are happy with the placing of the leaves, and make any necessary adjustments.

The position of the embellishments creates space and frames the face beautifully.

Attaching the leaves and the flowers

First sew the beads and felt leaves to the roses, using a thread to match the ribbon flowers. Then sew the roses in position onto the band. Make sure all the thread ends are sewn in securely before cutting off.

Tying the garland

Wrap the garland around your head in your chosen style. As the ric rac is not slippery, tying it in a simple bow at the back should keep it in place.

DESIGN INSPIRATIONS

Try different colours of ribbon roses, or replace with knitted and crochet flowers (see Pretty Knitty Flowers).

•

If flowers aren't you, simply change the roses for fabric-covered buttons (see Cover Up).

•

Try out different types of tie – leather thong or vintage lace, for example.

•

To wear the garland in the style of a Grecian goddess, place it at the back of your neck; taking an end in each hand, bring the ends up to the front of your head, cross over and tie in a bow at the back of the neck.

SUPER SNUG TIEBACK

These knitted and crochet tieback headbands are perfect for those days when your hair is misbehaving and needs to be kept perfectly in place. Both are worked in basic stitches with a little bit of increasing for the section that runs across the top of the head, giving you a great base to add embellishments.

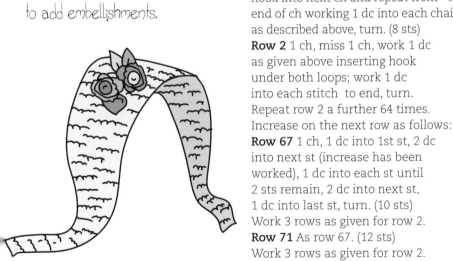

Materials (for each band)

- 50g (1¾oz) ball of 4ply (fine-weight) or DK (light-weight) cotton-based yarn
- 3mm (D3) crochet hook or 3.25mm (size 3) knitting needle

Working the crochet band

With 3mm (D3) hook and yarn colour of your choice, make 8 chain (ch) plus 1 turning ch.
Row 1 Miss 1st ch, insert hook into 2nd ch from hook, * yarn round hook (yrh) and draw through (2 loops on hook), yrh and pull through both loops on hook (1 loop on hook) – 1 double crochet (dc) has been worked. Insert hook into next ch and repeat from * to end of ch working 1 dc into each chain as described above, turn. (8 sts)
Row 2 1 ch, miss 1 ch, work 1 dc as given above inserting hook under both loops; work 1 dc into each stitch to end, turn.
Repeat row 2 a further 64 times.
Increase on the next row as follows:
Row 67 1 ch, 1 dc into 1st st, 2 dc into next st (increase has been worked), 1 dc into each st until 2 sts remain, 2 dc into next st, 1 dc into last st, turn. (10 sts)
Work 3 rows as given for row 2.
Row 71 As row 67. (12 sts)
Work 3 rows as given for row 2.
Row 75 As row 67. (14 sts)
Work 49 rows as given for row 2.
Decrease on the next row as follows:
Row 125 1 ch, 1 dc into 1st st, miss next st, 1 dc into each st until 2 sts remain, miss next st, 1 dc into last st. (12 sts)
Work 3 rows as given for row 2.

Row 129 As row 125. (10 sts)
Work 3 rows as given for row 2.
Row 133 As row 125. (8 sts)
Work a further 66 rows as given for row 2. Break off yarn and pull through loop to secure.

Working the knitted band

With 3.25mm (size 3) needles and chosen yarn colour cast on 8 sts.
Row 1 Knit to end.
Rows 2–120 As row 1.
Increase on the next row as follows:
Row 121 K1, knit into the front and back of the next stitch (inc 1), knit until 2 sts remain on left- hand needle (LHN), inc 1 as given at beginning of row, k1. (10 sts)
Work 5 rows knit.
Row 127 As row 121. (12 sts)
Work 3 rows knit.
Row 131 As row 121. (14 sts)
Work 15 rows knit.
Row 147 K1, knit 2 together through the back of the loops (k2tog tbl) by inserting needle through the back of the next 2 sts, knit until 3 sts on the LHN, then knit 2 together (k2tog) by inserting needle through the next 2 sts, k1. (12 sts)
Work 3 rows knit.
Row 151 As row 147. (10 sts)
Work 5 rows knit.
Row 157 As row 147. (8 sts)
Work a further 120 rows in knit. Cast (bind) off. Break off yarn and pull through loop to secure.

If you would like to add colour and pattern to the tiebacks, simply choose a self-striping yarn for maximum effect with minimum effort.

Finishing off

Sew in loose ends of yarn on the wrong side of the headband. Decorate with the embellishments of your choosing.

To keep your decoration detachable and ring the changes day by day, use a safety pin to secure embellishments to the band.

DESIGN INSPIRATIONS

The Super Snug Tieback makes the perfect projects to use up yarn odds and ends, simply by introducing a few stripes to the basic band.

•

Explore using different yarns, but if you use a thicker yarn remember to use a larger needle or hook and reduce the amount of rows worked.

•

Confident knitters could try using a different stitch pattern, for example moss (seed) stitch.

•

Crocheters could work the pattern substituting treble crochet for the double crochet.

FAB FABRIC TIEBACKS

Choose from two great fabric tiebacks. Both are long enough to be tied to the front or the back of the head depending on your mood.

Materials

For the skinny band
- 10cm (4in) wide fabric strip, approx. 110cm (43in) long
- Adhesive mending tape (optional)

For the broad band
- Two 10cm (4in) wide fabric strips, approx. 110cm (43in) long

Decorate a plain fabric with motifs to create your own patterned fabric – attach using fusible webbing (see Flower Cut Outs), or stitch by hand.

The broad band has a wider section at its centre, but its narrow ties means it too sits perfectly around the head.

Making the broad band

Using the diagram provided as a guide, cut out the broad band template to the correct size (Fig. 1).

Iron your fabric strips to remove any creases before starting. With wrong side up and facing you, pin the broad band template to one of the fabric strips and draw around the outline using a ball-point pen or fabric pen. Carefully cut around the marked line. Repeat to cut a second broad band from the remaining fabric strip.

Pin the two fabric pieces right sides together but leave the short ends unpinned for turning through after stitching.

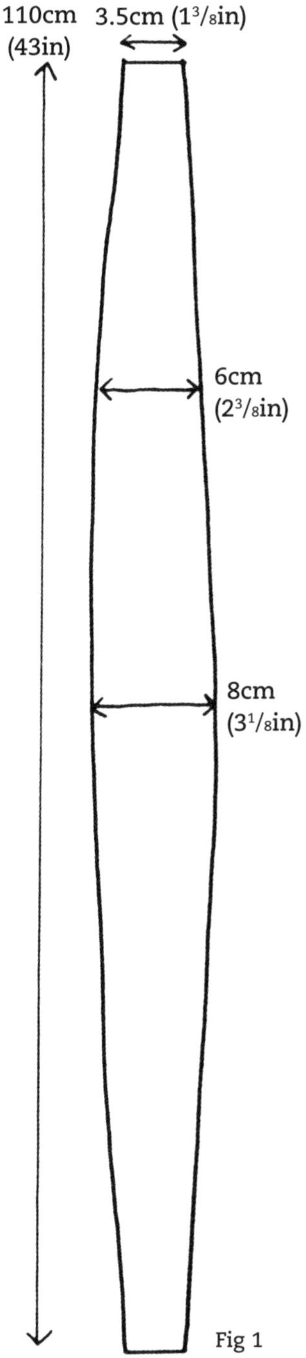

110cm (43in)   **3.5cm (1³/₈in)**

6cm (2³/₈in)

8cm (3¹/₈in)

Fig 1

Machine stitch along the pinned edges approx. 2cm (¾in) in from the edge (or backstitch by hand-stitch) Turn the fabric the right way out and press to flatten out the seams. Tuck in the open ends and sew closed using a hem stitch or backstitch.

Making the skinny band

Iron your fabric strip to remove any creases before starting. Fold over the ends by approx. 2cm (¾in) and press with a steam iron to fix the folds in place. Now hem the long edges: fold over by approx. 1cm (³/₈in) and press; fold over the folded edges by approx. 1cm (³/₈in) and press once again (Fig. 2). Fold the band in half lengthways to bring the long edges together and press once more (Fig. 3).

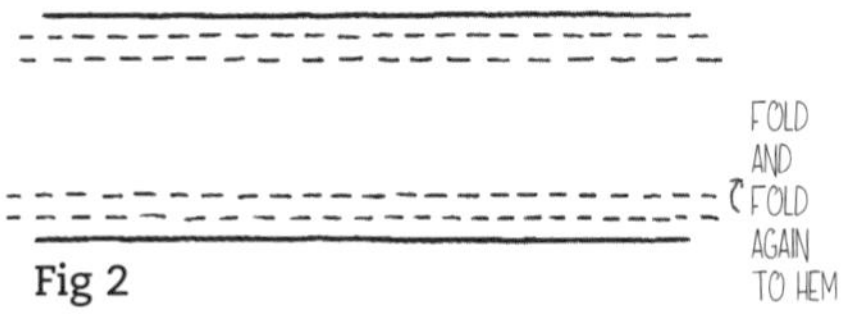

FOLD AND FOLD AGAIN TO HEM

Fig 2

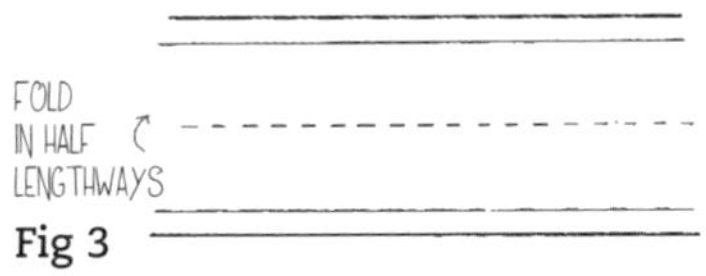

FOLD IN HALF LENGTHWAYS

Fig 3

Make sure you match the edges exactly – it's best to take your time to get this right, and an ironing board makes an ideal surface on which to work.

To finish with adhesive mending tape
This is a sticky strip that bonds fabrics together quickly and easily, providing a firmly joined finish without the need to heat – it's a

bit like a double-sided adhesive tape suitable for fabrics. Open out the folded fabric band and run the sticky side of the tape around the edges facing you. Peel off the tape backing, close the band and press down the edges to secure. Do check the edges to make sure that they are firmly joined – you can work around the edges with hem stitch if required (see Techniques). Run an iron along the edge to flatten.

To finish with machine stitching
Pin the edges of the folded fabric band together and stitch all around the outer edge using a straight stitch.

To finish with hand-stitching
Pin the edges of the folded fabric band together and stitch all around the outer edge using a hem stitch.

DESIGN INSPIRATIONS
For the broad band, use different prints for the top and bottom fabric strips.

•

Embellish printed fabrics with accent embroidery, such as an embroidered daisy stitch pattern for a floral print or a running stitch to outline motifs in a contrast colour.

•

Gather together a selection of buttons to tone with your fabric choice and play about with their placement on the band – slightly off centre and gathered in a group works well.

WOVEN WONDERS

A simple crochet band provides the basic framework for these ever-changing tiebacks. Use a prepared fabric strip, or a length of ribbon, and weave it in and out of the crochet sleeve — change your fabric insert to match your outfit.

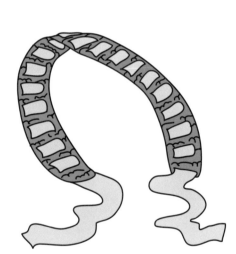

Materials

- 50g (1¾oz) ball of 4ply (fine-weight) or DK (light-weight) cotton based yarn
- 3mm (D3) crochet hook
- 10cm (4in) wide cotton fabric strip, approx. 1m (39¼in) long
- Safety pin

Working the crochet sleeve

With 3mm (D3) crochet hook and yarn colour of your choice, make 8 chain (ch) plus 1 turning ch.
Row 1 Miss 1st ch, insert hook into 2nd ch from hook, * yarn round hook (yrh) and draw through (2 loops on hook), yrh and pull through both loops on hook (1 loop on hook) – 1 double crochet (dc) has been worked. Insert hook into next ch and repeat from * to end of ch working 1 dc into each chain as described above, turn. (8 sts)
Row 2 1 ch, miss 1 ch, work 1 dc as given above inserting hook under both loops; work 6 ch, miss 6 dc, work 1 dc into last dc, turn. Repeat row 2 a further 59 times.
Next row 1 ch, miss 1 ch, work 1 dc into each stitch to end, turn. Break off yarn and pull through loop to secure.

For a wider band, add stitches and work the pattern as given – for example, work 12 ch for the base, then in multiples of 10.

Finishing off the crochet sleeve

Sew in the loose ends of yarn on the wrong side. Pin out onto an ironing board using glass-headed pins, making sure that the width of the strip is even. Place a damp tea towel over the crochet strip and press gently with a steam iron. Allow the crochet strip to dry completely before removing the pins.

Run a clean tea towel under the cold tap and wring out well so that it is just damp but not dripping wet.

Making the fabric insert

Iron your fabric strip to remove any creases before starting. Fold over the ends by approx. 2cm (¾in) and press with a steam iron to fix the folds in place. Now hem the long edges: fold over by 1cm (⅜in) and press; fold over the folded edges by 1cm (⅜in) once again and press. Fold the fabric strip in half lengthways so that the hemmed edges meet; press along the length. Because the fabric is cotton and has been pressed with a steam iron, the strip should keep its shape and will not unravel; however, if you choose to, you can machine stitch the edges together, or use a hem stitch to secure by hand.

For a no-sew version, use a ribbon insert – try a sheer organza or a classic tartan. It is important to make sure that the width of your ribbon is slightly narrower than the gaps you will be weaving in and out of as if it is too wide it will not sit flat in the insert.

Making up

Attach the safety pin to one of the short edges of the fabric strip (this will make the weaving of the fabric strip insert in and out of the crochet sleeve easier to do).

Place the crochet sleeve in front of you with the right side facing you. Working from one end of the sleeve, bring the fabric insert up through the first gap, over the top of the first set of 6 ch and back down, and continue to weave in and out in this way to the very end of the crochet sleeve (Fig. 1).

Fold the fabric insert in half and slide the crochet sleeve up the fabric strip until the centre of the crochet sleeve reaches the centre of the insert. Pin the ends of the crochet sleeve to the fabric insert and sew into position to secure.

Fig 1

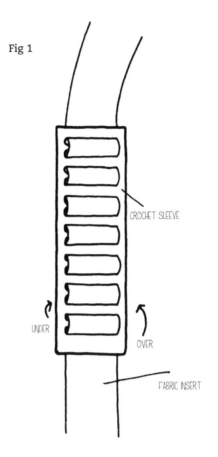

CROCHET SLEEVE

UNDER

OVER

FABRIC INSERT

Make several different fabric inserts to coordinate with all your favourite outfits. If you do want to be able to change over the fabric insert, you must not sew the crochet sleeve in place.

DESIGN INSPIRATIONS

Experiment with different yarns, but if you use a thicker yarn you will need to go up a hook size, and as the band will be wider and longer, you may want to reduce the amount of rows worked.

•

To give the crochet sleeve a different look work in a stripe pattern, but remember, if you work a 2-row strip, one of the colours will be covered by the insert.

•

Check out your local haberdashery store for other insert options – an open lacy trim or a jumbo ric rac braid would give an interesting effect.

•

You can use two or three finer ribbons for the insert; weave the lengths in and out alternately to add to the woven effect of the band.

•

For extra embellishment, stitch a few buttons onto the finished tieback.

DAISY CHAIN

For this flower garland, each daisy is constructed individually, made from craft wire, felt fabric and a button. The flowers are designed so that they slot together — just like a daisy chain — so that you can make the garland as long as you want.

Materials

- Felt fabric: white, yellow and green
- Large two-hole flat-back buttons
- One roll of 1.2mm sterling-plated craft wire
- Round-nose pliers

Making the flower centre

Cut a length of wire approx. 30cm (12in). Fold over by approx. 5cm (2in) at one end and insert through the holes of the button (Fig. 1), and twist to secure.

Fig 1

To cover the button cut a circle of yellow felt fabric approx. 1.5cm (⅝in) wider than the button. Using sewing thread, work a running stitch all around the edge of the circle approx. 5mm (¼in) in from the edge. Place the felt circle over the button and pull the thread ends tight to gather the fabric around the underside of the button. Work a few backstitches to secure, and leave a long length of thread to secure the stem covering.

Covering the flower stem

Cut a strip of green felt fabric approx. 5mm (¼in) wide. Using the long length of thread left hanging at the base of the flower, work a couple of backstitches to secure the strip to the underside of the button.

If you cut the green felt strip too narrow it will snap, but if it is too thick it won't sit nicely around the wire.

Wrap the felt strip tightly around the wire, slightly overlapping each time. Work your way carefully down towards the ends of the wire. When you have approx. 1cm (⅜in) of wire left to cover, bend the wire up to form a loop at the bottom, and twist the uncovered part of the wire around the stem (Fig. 2).

Wrap the felt around the stem to cover the twist. Once the wire stem has been completely covered, work a few backstitches to secure the felt in place.

TWIST

Fig 2

Making the flower petals

Cut a rectangle approx. 8 x 5cm (3⅛ x 2in) from the white felt fabric. Fold in half lengthways and pin the long edges together.

Using sharp scissors and working your way from right to left, cut from the folded edge down towards the pinned edge, allowing approx. 5mm (¼in) between each cut and leaving approx. 1cm (⅜in) uncut at the pinned edge (Fig. 3).

You will find that the pins will prevent your scissors from cutting straight through, but do be careful.

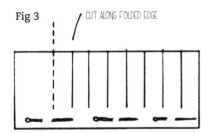

Fig 3   CUT ALONG FOLDED EDGE

Keeping the white felt fabric folded in half, roll it into a tube. With the petals to the top, pin and stitch at the bottom to secure. Work a running stitch around the base and pull tight to gather in the bottom and open out the petals.

Finishing the daisy

Insert the loop end of the stem down through the centre of the petals so that the flower is formed with the button sitting towards the top. Stitch the base of the petals to the stem.

Making the garland

Make as many daisies as you need to fit around your head. Slot the daisies together – just like a daisy chain – to make the garland.

DESIGN INSPIRATIONS

Experiment with using different types of fabric to create the rolled flower – woven fabrics will fray to give you a shabby chic look.

•

Embellish the button centres with beads or embroidery – a mix of French knots and small seed beads would work well.

•

You could create another style of flower shape – for example, try cutting individual heart-shape petals and sew them together around the button base.

TECHNIQUES

Covering a Headband

Many of the projects featured use a shop-bought plastic headband as the base. These should be covered with felt and/or fabric as the project instructions advise.

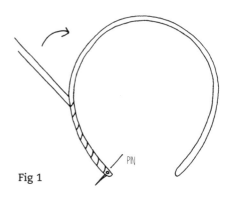

Fig 1

SIMPLE COVERED HEADBAND

Using felt to cover a headband is simplest and works best on narrow headbands. You can choose to either sew or glue on the fabric, and both methods are described below.

Materials

- Fine headband approx. 5mm (¼in) wide
- Black felt fabric rectangle approx. 22.9 x 30.5cm (size as sold)
- Fabric glue (for no sew version)

Wrapping and sewing on fabric

Cut three or four strips approx. 1.5cm (⁵⁄₈in) wide from the felt fabric. Holding the band in one hand, use your writing hand to begin to wrap the felt fabric strip around the leg of the band, securing the end with a glass-headed pin. Continue to wrap the felt around the band (Fig. 1), gently stretching it for a snug fit – do not pull too tightly or the strip will snap!

When you come to the end of a strip, take the next strip and overlap by approx. 1cm (³⁄₈in), securing the ends with a glass-headed pin. Continue wrapping until the band is completely covered. Thread a sharp sewing needle with black cotton thread and use a backstitch or whipping stitch to secure the felt fabric ends marked by the pins.

If using a different coloured felt, use a thread to match it so that the stitches won't show.

Wrapping and gluing on fabric

Work exactly as above, but instead of securing the fabric ends with glass-headed pins, use glue. You will need to wait for the glue to dry before continuing with each fabric strip. To give an even finish to the band, I would recommend working just a few stitches to ensure the edges of felt fabric lie flat and do not poke up.

You can use ribbon or other fabrics for this covering method – slippery ribbons will need to be secured with pins every few winds around the band, and woven fabrics may fray, which adds an interesting texture.

FABRIC COVERED HEADBAND

The directions given are to cover a 5mm (¼in) wide headband, but you can use this method to cover any width of straight headband – just make sure the fabric strip is wide enough to overlap when wrapped around the band and take into allowance the 5mm (¼in) hem.

Materials

- Fine headband approx. 5mm (¼in) wide
- Cotton fabric strip approx. 42 x 10cm (16½ x 4in)
- Fusible webbing strip approx. 42 x 4cm (16½ x 1½in)
- Interfacing strip approx. 42 x 4cm (16½ x 1½in)

Preparing the fabric

Spray the cotton fabric strip with water or dampen by running under the tap. Press with a steam iron. This will ensure that the fabric doesn't twist slightly.

Measure and mark a 4cm (1½in) wide strip down the middle of the fabric strip, wrong side facing. Place the rough side of the fusible webbing strip onto the marked rectangle and press; allow to cool, then peel off the backing. Place the interfacing strip on top and press again to fix.

Adding a fusible web/interfacing strip to the fabric adds structure and makes it easier to sew together.

Measure the length of the headband – the average is approx. 38cm (15in); fold up the short ends of the fabric strip to match the headband length. Next fold in a hem of approx. 5mm (¼in) along the side edges. Press all hems to keep the folds in place.

If ribbon is used, no hemming is required. Satin ribbon is slightly slippery, so if it has a pattern you will need to be careful to keep it straight.

Covering the headband

Place each leg of the headband under the folds at the short ends of the fabric (Fig. 1), using glass-headed pins to secure if necessary.

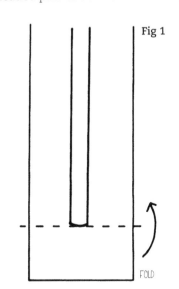

Fig 1

Working your way from the right leg of the headband to the left, fold the fabric around the headband and secure with pins (Fig. 2). Stitch the fabric together using an invisible hemstitch, removing the pins as you go.

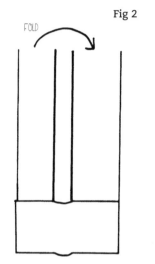

Fig 2

You can thicken or bulk up a headband by wrapping it first with felt fabric (see Simple Covered Headband) before covering it in fabric.

Working Stitches

Here are the stitches that you will need to make up and embellish the projects featured in this book.

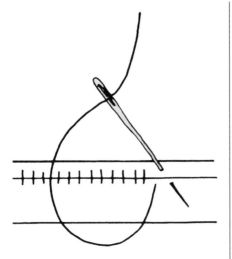

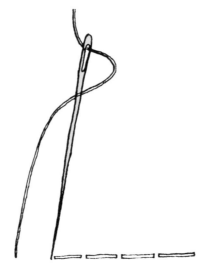

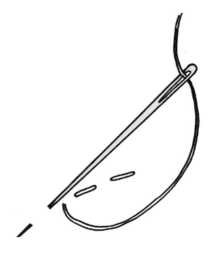

Hem stitch (aka whipping stitch)

A basic over-and-over stitch that can be used to hem almost invisibly. Insert the needle into the folded fabric, slightly catching one side of the fabric and bringing it out slightly behind the folded hem, catching the other side of the fabric as you go. Repeat until the hem is completed.

Backstitch

Working from right to left, bring the needle up through the fabric at the required position. Make a stitch, and insert the needle back into the fabric to double back on itself, bringing it back up beyond the stitch just made. To repeat, insert the needle into the fabric at the point of the first stitch.

Running stitch

Bring the needle up through the fabric, make a stitch, and bring the needle down through the fabric again. You can take more than one stitch on your needle at a time, but make sure that your stitches are the same size and equally spaced. You are aiming for the space in between the stitches to be approx. half the length of the stitches.

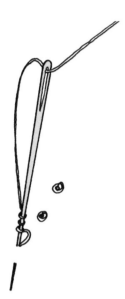

French knots

Bring the thread up from the back of the fabric to the required position. Hold the needle down with the left thumb and wrap the thread around it three or four times. Hold the thread tightly and reinsert the needle as close as possible to where the thread originally came out (do not go back into exactly the same hole as the knot will be lost). Pull the thread through to the back of the fabric and secure if working a single French knot, or bring the needle back out to the front of the fabric where you want the next French knot to be.

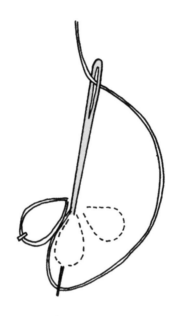

Daisy chain

Bring the thread out at the required position. Make a loop with the thread slightly bigger than the desired petal size, and hold the loop down with your thumb. Reinsert the needle where the thread originally came out, and bring the needle out to the front of the fabric at the required length of the petal. Pull the thread through, and then back into the fabric over the top of the petal loop, bringing the needle back out at the base of the petal just worked. Repeat this process to work the required number of petals.

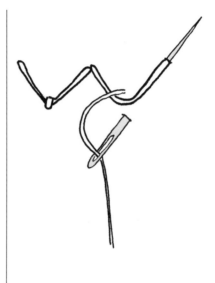

Fly stitch

Bring the needle through to the front of the fabric (top left). Holding the thread down with your left thumb, insert the needle to the right at the same level. Bring the needle back up through the fabric, slightly down from the original stitch and to the inside of the looped thread. Catch the loop to bring the needle back down to the wrong side of the fabric to make a 'V' shape, and back out top right ready to work the next stitch.

Knitting Basics

This section will be very useful to those new to knitting, helping you to work the projects in the book. It is best to read these pages before you start working on a project.

Knitting gauge

The gauge or tension is the number of stitches and rows needed to knit 2.5cm (1in). Most knitting projects recommend that you knit a gauge square before starting the project to ensure you knit it up to the correct size and fit. The gauge is given over 10.2cm (4in). To check your gauge, knit a square at least 15.5cm (6in), using the stated yarn, needle size and stitch. Measure the square to check your gauge is correct; if it isn't, you will need to knit tighter or looser. Alternatively, use a size smaller or larger knitting needle.

Measure in the middle of the square rather than the edges, as these may be distorted.

Knitting abbreviations

Abbreviations are used in knitting patterns to shorten commonly used terms so that the instructions are a manageable length. The following is a list of the abbreviations used when making the projects in this book.

approx	approximately
cm	centimetre(s)
DK	double knitting
g	gram(s)
inc	increase(s)/increasing
in(s)	inch(es)
k	knit
k2tog	knit 2 stitches together (1 stitch decreased)
k2tog tbl	knit 2 stitches together through back of loops (1 stitch decreased)
LHN	left-hand needle
mm	millimetres
oz	ounces
ss	slip stitch
st(s)	stitch(es)
tbl	through back of loop
*	repeat directions following * as many times as indicated or to end of row

Casting on

To begin knitting, you need to work a foundation row of stitches and this is called casting on. There are several ways to cast on stitches and a cable cast-on method is described here.

1 Take two needles and make a slip knot about 15.5cm (6in) from the end of the yarn on one needle. Hold this needle in your left hand. Insert the right-hand needle knitwise into the loop on the left-hand needle and wrap the yarn around the tip.

2 Pull the yarn through the loop to make a stitch but do not drop the stitch off the left-hand needle.

3 Slip the new stitch on to the left-hand needle by inserting the left-hand needle into the front of the loop from right to left. You will now have two stitches on the left-hand needle.

4 Insert the right-hand needle between the two stitches on the left-hand needle and wrap the yarn around the tip. Pull the yarn back through between the two stitches and place it on the left-hand needle, as in step 3. Repeat until you have cast on the stitches required.

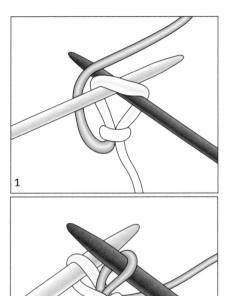

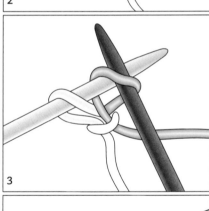

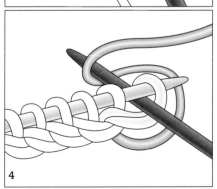

Knit stitch (k)

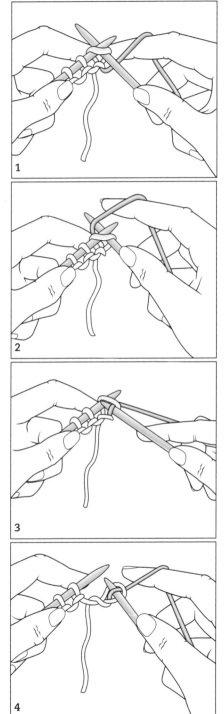

This is the simplest stitch of all. Each stitch is created with a four-step process. Hold the yarn at the back of the work – this is the side facing away from you.

1 Place the needle with the cast-on stitches in your left hand, insert the right-hand needle into the front of the first stitch on the left-hand needle from left to right.

2 Take the yarn around and under the point of the right-hand needle.

3 Draw the new loop on the right-hand needle through the stitch on the left-hand needle.

4 Slide the stitch off the left-hand needle. This has formed one knit stitch on the right-hand needle.
   Repeat until all stitches on the left-hand needle have been transferred to the right-hand needle. This is the end of the row. Swap the right-hand needle into your left hand and begin the next row in exactly the same way.

Knit stitch — continental method

In this method the right-hand needle moves to catch the yarn; the yarn is held at the back of the work (the side facing away from you) and is released by the index finger of the left hand.

1 Hold the needle with the cast on stitches in your left hand and the yarn over your left index finger. Insert the right-hand needle into the front of the stitch from left to right.

2 Move the right-hand needle down and across the back of the yarn.

3 Pull the new loop on the right-hand needle through the stitch on the left-hand needle, using the right index finger to hold the new loop if needed.

4 Slip the stitch off the left-hand needle. One knit stitch is completed.

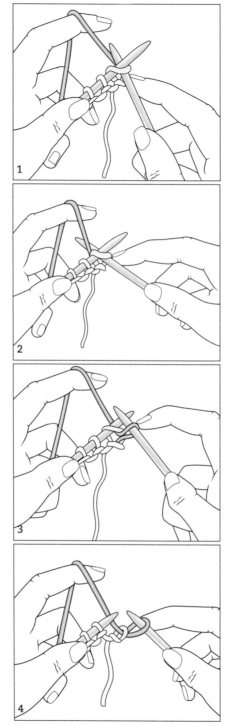

Knit into front and back to increase 1

An easy way to increase one stitch is by working into the front and back of the same stitch. Knit into the front of the stitch as usual. Do not slip the stitch off the left-hand needle but knit into it again through the back of the loop, and then slip the original stitch off the left-hand needle. You can make a stitch on a purl row in the same way but purling into the front and back of the stitch.

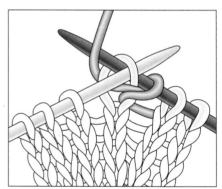

K2tog tbl to decrease 1

1 Slip two stitches knitwise one at a time from the left-hand needle to the right-hand needle (they will be twisted).

2 Insert the left-hand needle from left to right through the fronts and knit together as one stitch (k2tog tbl).

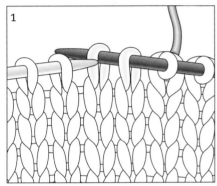

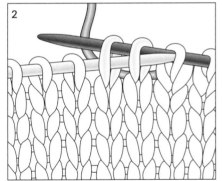

Casting off

Casting (binding) off links stitches together so that they cannot unravel and secures stitches when a piece of knitting is complete.

1 Knit the first two stitches. Insert the point of the left-hand needle into the front of the first stitch on the right-hand needle.

2 Lift the first stitch on the right-hand needle over the second stitch and off the needle.

3 One stitch is left on the right-hand needle as pictured. Repeat in this way until all the stitches on the left-hand needle have been cast off to leave just one stitch remaining on the right-hand needle. To finish, cut the yarn (leaving a length long enough to sew or weave in) and pass the end through the last stitch. Slip the stitch off the needle and pull the yarn end to tighten it.

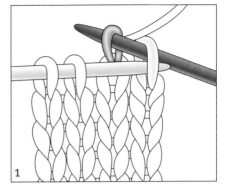

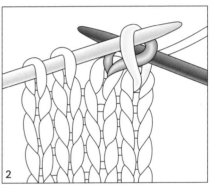

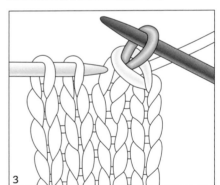

Crochet Basics

This section will be very useful if you are new to the craft of crochet, helping you to work the projects in the book. It is best to read these pages before you start working on a project.

Crochet abbreviations

Abbreviations are used to shorten commonly used terms to make instructions a manageable length. You should be aware that crochet terms in the US differ from those in the UK. This can be confusing as the same terms are used to refer to different stitches under each system. The list below gives a translation of UK to US terms as used.

UK term	US term
double crochet	single crochet
treble crochet	double crochet

Slip knot

Create a loop with the yarn, making sure that the tail of the yarn is dangling behind the loop. Insert the crochet hook through the loop, moving under the tail and back out of the loop. Grab the tail with the hook and pull to create the slip knot on the crochet hook.

Chain stitch (ch)

Chain stitch can be worked in various ways, as a single stitch, or in a row to form a long chain, or joined into a circle.

1 Tie a slip knot in the working end of your yarn and place the loop on the crochet hook. Wrap the yarn clockwise over the hook and then pull the yarn through the loop on the hook to form a fresh loop. This is one chain stitch.

2 Repeat the process until you have as many chain stitches as needed.

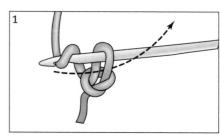

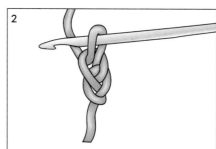

Double crochet (dc)

The double crochet stitch is the shortest of the crochet stitches.

1 To make the stitch, insert your hook under the top two strands of the stitch beneath (or, if you're working into the foundation row, insert the hook into the centre of the chain stitch). Wrap the yarn over the hook and pull the yarn through.

2 Then wrap the yarn over the hook again and pull it through both the loops on the hook. This forms one double crochet stitch.

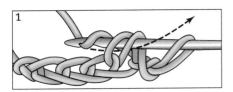

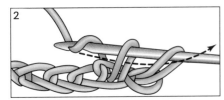

Treble crochet

1 When working treble crochet, first wrap the yarn around the hook from back to front before inserting it into the work.

2 Now wrap the yarn around the hook from back to front and pull the yarn through the work on the hook. Now there will be three loops on the hook.

3 Wrap the yarn around the hook from back to front and pull through the remaining two loops on the hook to complete the treble crochet.

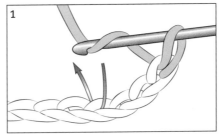

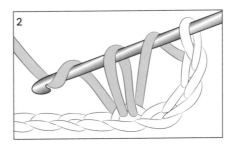

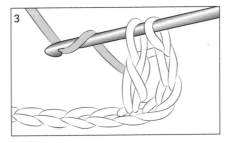

Slip stitch (ss)

This stitch adds no height to the work and is generally used to move the hook to a new place without cutting yarn. Insert the hook into the work at the required position. Wrap the yarn around the hook from back to front and pull the yarn through both the work and the loop on the hook to complete the slip stitch.

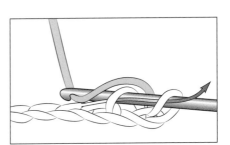

TEMPLATES

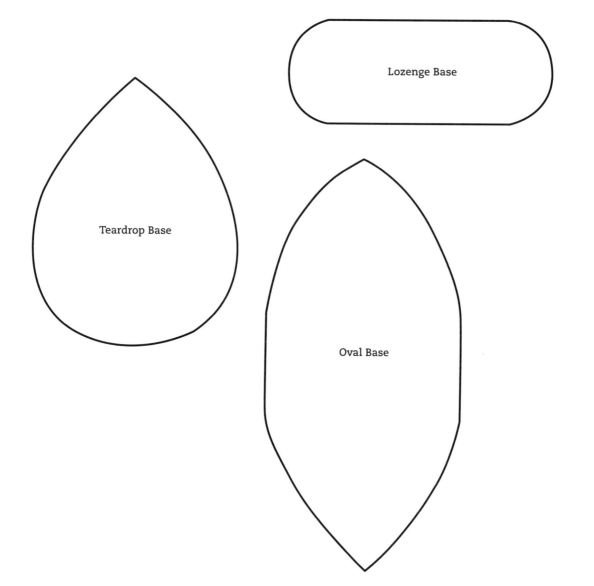

Lozenge Base

Teardrop Base

Oval Base

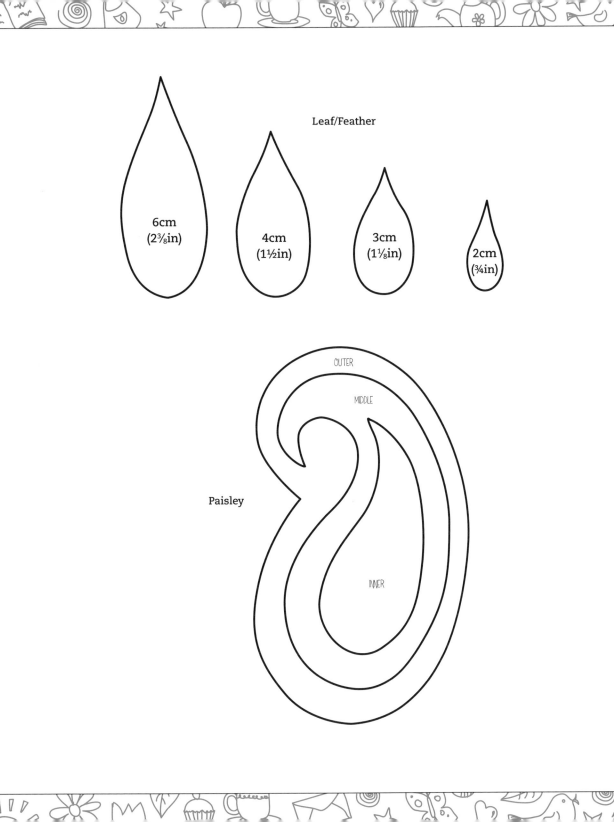

Leaf/Feather

6cm
(2⅜in)

4cm
(1½in)

3cm
(1⅛in)

2cm
(¾in)

Paisley

OUTER

MIDDLE

INNER

Suppliers

Creative buttons and self-cover buttons are Prym products, available through Coats Crafts UK, who also supply felt fabric in a range of colours.

Coats Crafts UK
Green Lane Mill
Holmfirth
West Yorkshire
England
HD9 2DX

Frogging trims can be bought from independent haberdasheries. Those used for Nautical Chic were manufactured by:

W. Williams & Sons Ltd
Regent House
1 Thane Villas
London
England
N7 7PH

Author's acknowledgements

I would like to thank everybody for their help and support in creating this fantastic book. Special thanks to Rowan and Coats Crafts UK for supplying the lovely materials used for the projects, and to my ever so patient and loving partner, Andy Daly, for supplying me with constant care and attention throughout. Thank you – I couldn't have done this without you all!

About the author

Carol Meldrum is a textile designer, workshop tutor and author of many popular knit and crochet titles. She was taught to knit, crochet and sew at a young age by her mum and grandma. Since graduating from Duncan of Jordanstone College of Art in Dundee, Carol has worked in the textile industry as a designer for many high-street fashion outlets as well as internationally-renowned hand-knit label Rowan, and her unique take on all things textile can be found online and in selected boutique shops in Scotland.

Carol is a successful workshop tutor travelling throughout the UK to teach all aspects of knit and crochet in an informal environment, to both groups and individuals. Her main goal is to give others the confidence to create handmade objects of their own, sharing skills that have been handed down through generations to produce new and exciting projects that will inspire others to do the same. She lives in Glasgow, Scotland.

Index

A DAVID & CHARLES BOOK
© F&W Media International, Ltd 2012

David & Charles is an imprint of F&W Media International, Ltd
Brunel House, Forde Close, Newton Abbot, TQ12 4PU, UK

F&W Media International, Ltd is a subsidiary of F+W Media, Inc
10151 Carver Road, Cincinnati OH45242, USA

Text and designs copyright © Carol Meldrum 2012
Layout and photography © F&W Media International, Ltd 2012

First published in the UK and US in 2012
Digital edition published in 2012

ISBN-13: 978-1-4463-0192-0 paperback
ISBN-10: 1-4463-0192-3 paperback

ISBN-13: 978-1-4463-5611-1 e-pub
ISBN-10: 1-4463-5611-6 e-pub

ISBN-13: 978-1-4463-5610-4 PDF
ISBN-10: 1-4463-5610-8 PDF

Printed in China by Toppan Leefung Printing Ltd
Brunel House, Forde Close, Newton Abbot, TQ12 4PU, UK

10 9 8 7 6 5 4 3 2 1

Junior Acquisitions Editor Sarah Callard
Assistant Editor Grace Harvey
Project Editor Cheryl Brown
Creative Manager Prudence Rogers
Photographer Lorna Yabsley
Senior Production Controller Kelly Smith

F+W Media publishes high quality books on a wide range of subjects.
For more great book ideas visit: www.rucraft.co.uk